insight text guide

Thomas Caldwell

The Castle

Dir. Rob Sitch

First published in 2021.

Insight Publications Pty Ltd
3/350 Charman Road
Cheltenham VIC 3192
Australia
Tel: +61 3 8571 4950
Fax: +61 3 8571 0257
Email: books@insightpublications.com.au

www.insightpublications.com.au

A catalogue record for this book is available from the National Library of Australia

Dir. Rob Sitch's The Castle / Thomas Caldwell

Thomas Caldwell asserts the moral right to be identified as the author of this work.

ISBNs:
9781922525499 (print)
9781922525505 (digital)
9781922525512 (bundle: print + digital)

Cover design by Gisela Beer

Printed in Australia by Ligare

contents

CHARACTER MAP

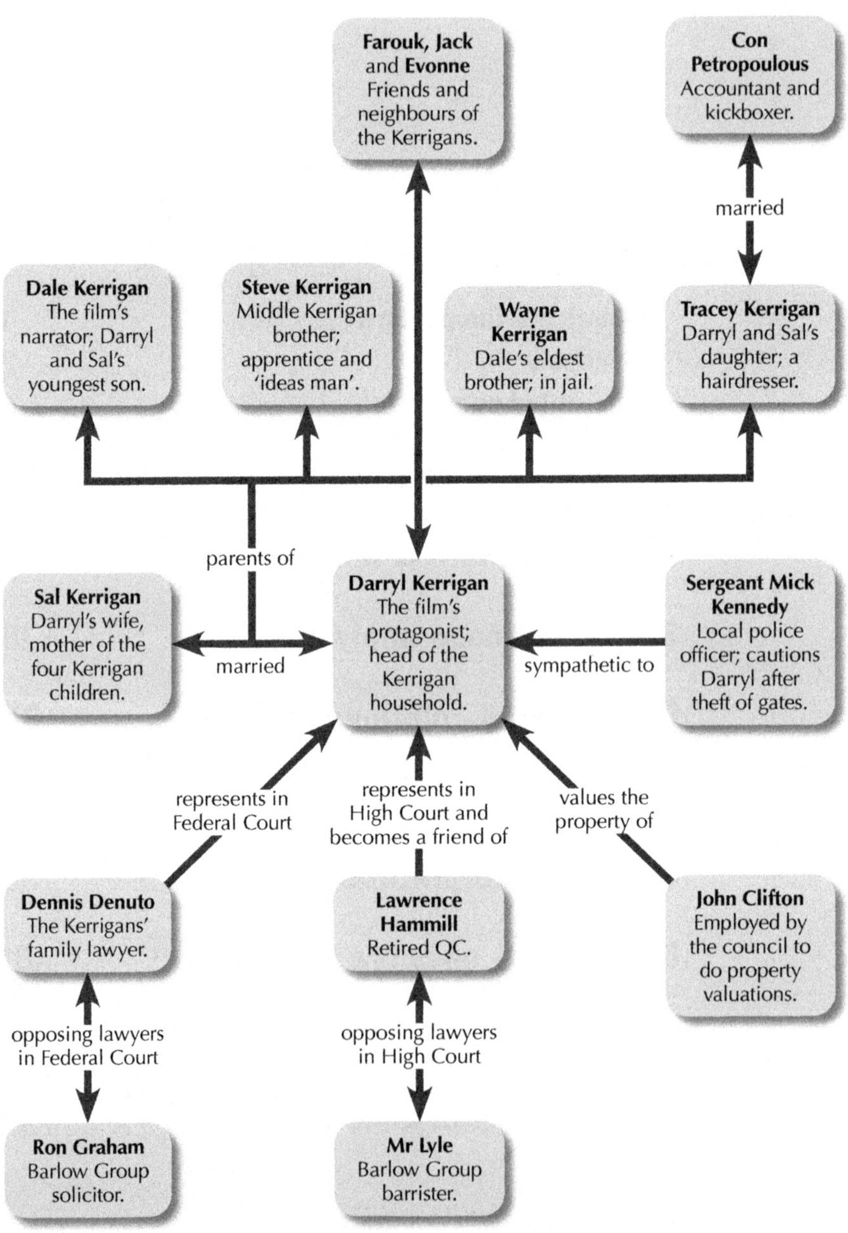

OVERVIEW

About the filmmakers

The low-budget independent Australian film *The Castle* was written and conceived by Santo Cilauro, Jane Kennedy, Tom Gleisner and Rob Sitch, with Sitch also credited as the director. While it is commonplace to credit the director as the 'author' of the film, in the case of *The Castle* it is presented as a collaborative project by Cilauro, Kennedy, Gleisner and Sitch through their Australian film and television production company, Working Dog.

Prior to forming Working Dog, Cilauro, Kennedy, Gleisner and Sitch had achieved considerable success on Australian television as members of the sketch comedy shows *The D Generation* (1986–89) and *The Late Show* (1992–93). Both shows were enormously influential and popular, and aired during a peak period for Australian television comedy, along with other hit sketch comedy shows such as *The Comedy Company* (1988–90) and *Fast Forward* (1989–92).

Working Dog was originally named Frontline Television Productions in reference to the team's first project, the satirical television comedy *Frontline* (1994–97) about a fictional commercial current affairs program. While the team's previous work had already given them a reputation for generating clever and absurd comedy through their ability to ridicule aspects of human behaviour and Australian society that had not often been scrutinised before, *Frontline* was even more groundbreaking. It presented a cynical and often savage behind-the-scenes look at how a current affairs television show operated, and is still highly acclaimed today.

After producing various other television shows, in 1997 the company made *The Castle*, their first feature film. *The Castle* follows the working-class Kerrigan family in their fight against a compulsory acquisition that would mean having to leave their beloved home so the neighbouring airport can be expanded. Invoking various legal principles about land rights, *The Castle* directly references famous Australian constitutional law cases, specifically the landmark Mabo case decision in 1992. The popularity and past successes of the Working Dog team led to high expectations for *The Castle*, and it proved to be an enormous critical and commercial success, winning three acting awards and the Best Original Screenplay award at the 1997 Australian Film Institute Awards.

Working Dog productions have left a huge mark on the Australian entertainment industry. Since *The Castle*, the Working Dog team has created numerous other television programs, including the talk show *The Panel* (1998–2004), political satire sitcoms *The Hollowmen* (2008) and *Utopia* (2014–19) and panel game show *Have You Been Paying Attention?* (2013–ongoing). Working Dog has also made the feature films *The Dish* (2000) and *Any Questions for Ben?* (2012).

Synopsis

The working-class Kerrigan family are the proud owners of a house situated next to an airport runway. The members of the family who live in the house are Darryl, his wife Sal and their sons Steve and Dale. They also have a daughter, Tracey, who recently married a man named Con, and one other son, Wayne, who is in jail for armed robbery. The family members are all extremely close and love their home.

After a council official comes to value their house, the Kerrigans receive a letter informing them that their property is being compulsorily acquired for an airport extension, which means they will have to move out. Their neighbours have received similar letters and they are all outraged. Darryl attempts to speak to the council, arguing that he does not want to leave despite the compensation being offered, but is informed he has no choice as a legally binding agreement between the airport authority and all levels of government allows them to take the land. Darryl then goes to see his solicitor, Dennis Denuto, and asks for his help, despite the fact that Dennis has no knowledge of this area of law. Dennis promises to look into the situation and Darryl is relieved, believing that the matter is resolved. The next day Darryl, Sal, Steve and Dale meet Tracey and Con at the airport after they arrive home from their honeymoon, and they all take a trip to their holiday house at Bonnie Doon.

Back home again, Darryl is confident that his hearing at the Administrative Appeals Tribunal will go well. However, despite having mounted a spirited argument for why it is unreasonable to take his house away from him, he loses the appeal on the grounds that there is no legal basis for his argument, as the airport is fully entitled to acquire his property. Darryl is devastated, but after consulting with his neighbours he decides to engage Dennis to represent him in court. Dennis is extremely reluctant because he thinks there is no way Darryl can win against the Barlow Group, the large and powerful corporation that is behind the airport expansion. Nevertheless, he agrees to help and gets to work.

A few days later the legal firm representing the Barlow Group sends a lawyer to negotiate with Dennis by offering more compensation. Darryl refuses. At the dinner table that night, Steve questions whether Darryl should actually have accepted the offer, but Sal recounts the story of the night she met Darryl and fell in love with him for his principles; it is those same principles that he is sticking to now by not backing down.

A man comes to the door with a thinly veiled threat that Darryl should accept the offer, but Steve chases the man away with a rifle. Later that night Steve's car is vandalised, so Darryl and Steve get their revenge by driving to the home of a Barlow Group executive and using Darryl's tow truck to rip the wrought-iron gates off. The next morning Mick, the local police sergeant, gives Darryl a friendly warning and turns a blind eye.

Darryl meets with his neighbours again and discovers they were also threatened, but still support Darryl's plan to hire Dennis for a legal appeal. However, when Dennis presents the case in the Federal Court he is completely out of his depth. During a break in proceedings, Darryl meets Lawrence (Laurie) by chance and the two men discuss their families and Darryl's case. Back inside the courtroom, the judge rules against Darryl, leaving him shattered.

Over dinner Darryl informs the rest of the family that they have two weeks to move out, which upsets everybody – including Wayne, when Dale delivers the news to him in prison. While packing to move, Darryl compares their situation to the First Nations people who also had their land taken away from them. All seems lost, but Lawrence makes a surprise visit, announcing that he is a retired Queen's Counsel (QC), he believes Darryl still has a case and he is willing to represent him for free. Three weeks later Lawrence, Dennis and Darryl are at the High Court of Australia where Lawrence and the opposing barrister, Mr Lyle, debate aspects of the Australian Constitution in relation to the case. During a short recess, Darryl delivers a powerful monologue outside the courthouse about the value of a home as opposed to a piece of land that can simply be bought and sold. Inspired by these words, Lawrence uses many of Darryl's ideas once he is back in the courtroom to sum up and ultimately win the case. That night there is a big party at the Kerrigan house to celebrate the victory.

The film ends with Dale telling the audience what happened to the characters thereafter: a happy ending for all.

Character summaries

Darryl Kerrigan

The blue-collar patriarch of the Kerrigan family, and the film's protagonist, whose attempt to prevent his home being acquired for an airport extension drives the narrative.

Sal Kerrigan

Darryl's loving and supportive wife, who loves doing crafts and has a part-time office job.

Dale Kerrigan

The youngest of Darryl and Sal's four children (all adults), who narrates the film. Dale still lives with his parents. He adores his family and is very sensitive.

Steve Kerrigan

Dale's older brother, who also lives in the family home. Steve is an apprentice mechanic, and is notable for inventing labour-saving but amateurish devices and using his negotiating skills to buy from the *Trading Post*.

Tracey Kerrigan

Darryl and Sal's only daughter, and Darryl's favourite child. She works as a hairdresser, recently got married and is on her honeymoon when the film begins.

Wayne Kerrigan

The eldest of the Kerrigan boys. Wayne is in prison for armed robbery, and is often shown wistfully looking at a family photo on his cell wall. His family still love him, especially Dale, who visits him regularly.

Con Petropoulous

Tracey's new husband, who works as an accountant and loves kickboxing. The Kerrigan family have welcomed him as one of their own.

Dennis Denuto

The Kerrigan family lawyer, who is well-meaning but hopelessly underqualified to argue Darryl's case in court and yet agrees to do so anyway.

Lawrence (Laurie) Hammill

A retired Queen's Counsel (QC) who befriends Darryl after a chance encounter despite their class differences, and takes over the case from Dennis.

Farouk, Jack and Evonne

Three of the neighbours whose homes are also to be compulsorily acquired. They support Darryl's attempt to fight the system.

John Clifton

A mild-mannered council worker who comes to do an evaluation of the Kerrigans' house.

Ron Graham

The smug solicitor who represents the Barlow Group during the Federal Court case.

Sergeant Mick Kennedy

The sympathetic local police officer who turns a blind eye to the removal of the gates but advises Darryl to act lawfully.

Mr Lyle

A condescending and insulting barrister who represents the Barlow Group during the High Court case.

BACKGROUND & CONTEXT

The Aussie battler

Darryl Kerrigan embodies the cultural and political construct of the Aussie battler, which has long been an idealised and romanticised image of working-class Australians who show resilience in the face of adversity and hardship. The idea of the Aussie battler was particularly prevalent in Australian society in the mid- to the late 1990s when the Liberal–National Coalition, under the leadership of John Howard, won the 1996 election. A lot of commentary at the time and since has argued that a factor in that win was the Coalition's use of 'Aussie battler' rhetoric to appeal to working-class Australians who traditionally voted for the opposing Australian Labor Party. During a 2004 radio interview, Howard roughly defined the battler as 'somebody who finds in life that they have to work hard for everything they get' and 'somebody who's not earning a huge income but somebody who is trying to better themselves' (Australian Associated Press 2004).

Larrikins, ockers and bogans

Variations of the Aussie battler as embodied by the Kerrigan family evolved from a long tradition of both romanticising and denigrating characteristics of Australian identity. The origins of terms such as 'larrikin', 'ocker' and 'bogan' are difficult to be precise about as they are colloquialisms that have evolved through common usage. The oldest of these terms is probably 'larrikin', which was originally used as a term of abuse to describe people with antisocial behaviour. However, during the twentieth century in Australia it evolved into an affectionate term for good-hearted people with a rebellious streak who do not stand on ceremony and are a bit reckless, all of which are traits that Darryl Kerrigan embodies.

The idea of the 'ocker' is somewhat similar to a larrikin, referring to an uncultivated Australian, but this slightly cruder term is more likely to be applied to people who are also heavy drinkers, generally crass, and chauvinistic – in a way that was once considered playful by some people, as opposed to discriminatory. It would not be accurate to describe the Kerrigans as ockers, but *The Castle* does reflect what had become known as an ocker comedy. While Australia was having a film renaissance in the 1970s and early 1980s with many groundbreaking art-house and mainstream films, low-budget and less refined Ozploitation films were also being made. These were often horror and action movies, but there was also a popular subgenre of ocker comedies in which uncouth, vulgar, distinctively Australian characters triumphed over authority, good taste and respectable institutions. Some of the most memorable ocker comedies include *Stork* (1971), *The Adventures of Barry McKenzie* (1972) and *Alvin Purple* (1973).

The concept of the 'bogan' as a subculture is shared with New Zealanders, but the term is generally believed to have become widely popular in Australia in the 1980s due to its use on the comedy sketch show *The Comedy Company* (which featured many contemporaries of the Working Dog team). Similar to the concept of the larrikin and ocker before it, the bogan was regarded as a low-class person with antisocial behaviour, whose stereotype was specifically that of a working-class person who lived in the outer suburbs, had bad taste, drank heavily and was not well educated. However, like larrikin and ocker, over time it has been embraced as a term of endearment to describe people who are defiantly outside of respectable middle-class Australian society.

Bogans are arguably thought of more affectionately than larrikins and ockers, as they more closely resemble underdogs who may have low social status and low incomes, but nevertheless mean well. In this regard they closely resemble the Aussie battler of Howard's Australia and the Kerrigan family in *The Castle*. However, it is worth stressing that all these terms – including the Aussie battler – are nebulous, conveying a general impression of a type of person rather than accurately describing a socioeconomic group.

Underdogs in Australian cinema

Given the degree to which many Australians see themselves as underdogs, it is not surprising that so much Australian cinema is about people of low status taking on a powerful opposition. While the Ozploitation films depicted ockers challenging social conventions, more mainstream films with similar concerns included *Breaker Morant* (1980) and *Gallipoli* (1981), war films in which Australian soldiers were at the mercy of English military command, and *Sunday Too Far Away* (1975), which portrayed the struggle for workers' rights among sheep shearers. Two of Australia's biggest blockbusters of the 1980s were *Crocodile Dundee* (1986) and *Young Einstein* (1988), which in many ways were more refined versions of the ocker comedies.

In the 1990s the majority of Australia's most successful and critically acclaimed films were also about low-status people (or in one case, a pig) triumphing over enormous odds, including *Strictly Ballroom* (1992), *The Adventures of Priscilla, Queen of the Desert* (1994), *Muriel's Wedding* (1994) and *Babe* (1995). Released in 1997, *The Castle* firmly embedded the concept of the underdog in the current mythology of the Aussie battler, and created a style of working-class suburban comedy that would be hugely influential, most notably seen in films such as *Kenny* (2006) and the television sitcom *Kath & Kim* (2002–07).

The Mabo case

The Castle was released five years after the landmark ruling in the Mabo case in 1992. This ten-year-long case was one of Australia's most significant and widely publicised court cases and the outcome led to the federal *Native Title Act 1993*, which established the framework for recognising the legal rights of First Nations peoples to have access to their traditional lands. It also acknowledged that First Nations peoples had occupied Australia prior to the arrival of European settlers.

The case is named after Eddie Koiki Mabo, one of four Meriam people from the Torres Strait Islands who in 1982 began a legal case for ownership of their traditional lands. One important aspect of the case was the overturning of the notion of terra nullius (a Latin term meaning 'land belonging to no-one'), which was a traditional colonial belief that prior to European settlement nobody owned Australian land and therefore it was justifiable for the British colonisers to claim it without recognising the existing rights of First Nations peoples.

Eddie Mabo had a background in campaigning for the rights of First Nations people and had extremely close ties with his community, in which he had become a prominent leader. While he was one of five plaintiffs in the ten-year case – beginning in the Queensland Supreme Court and finally concluding in the High Court of Australia – he became its figurehead and thus his name became synonymous with the historical ruling. Sadly, Eddie Mabo died at the age of fifty-six, only a few months before the High Court ruled in his and his fellow plaintiffs' favour. Eddie Mabo has since been recognised and honoured for his work in bringing First Nations peoples some justice and recognition by helping to overturn the myth of terra nullius. Referring to this case, or even the *Native Title Act*, simply as 'Mabo' has been commonplace for many years, so audiences who originally saw *The Castle* in 1997 would have known exactly what Dennis and other characters were referring to.

Greyhound racing

Greyhound racing has existed in Australia since 1927 and has long been associated with working-class communities. Owning greyhounds that are used for racing is one of many details in the film that identifies the Kerrigans as working class. In more recent times the industry has been accused of animal cruelty and greyhounds who have been rescued or retired from racing have become popular pets. In contrast to critical views of the industry, the Kerrigan dogs are depicted as being very much loved and cared for. To establish this, the greyhounds are introduced in the film in a medium close-up shot with Darryl looking at them affectionately.

The Trading Post

Throughout the film Steve is seen reading *The Trading Post,* a classified newspaper, founded in Melbourne in 1966, that predominantly listed various items for private sale. While the newspaper version is no longer published, it still exists online, providing a service similar to eBay, Gumtree and Amazon Marketplace. However, in 1997, when *The Castle* was released, and long before buying and selling online was a commonplace activity, *The Trading Post* was well established as a source of second-hand goods, ranging from the everyday to more obscure and strange items. Australian audiences at the time of the film's release would have at least heard of *The Trading Post* and been aware of its eclectic listings, which some people would browse simply for the entertainment value. The recurring joke of Steve finding bizarre items (jousting sticks, for example) and Darryl commenting that the seller is asking too much for them (dreamin') would have been a familiar scenario for many viewers. This is one of *The Castle*'s many amusing and original depictions of mundane aspects of Australian suburban life.

The Price Is Right

When Tracey is introduced, Dale's narration tells us that as well as having a certificate in hairdressing, Tracey made Darryl proud when she was on *The Price Is Right,* which was a popular game show that screened on and off in Australia in various formats from 1973 to 2012. During one of its more popular runs in the late 1990s it was hosted by television presenter Larry Emdur, who appears in the film's flashback sequence as himself as the show's host, with Tracey as a contestant. The scene captures the excitement that a working-class family like the Kerrigans may have felt by having a family member on such a high-profile prime-time television game show.

Hey Hey It's Saturday

Hey Hey It's Saturday was an enormously popular Australian variety show that ran on the Nine Network from 1971 to 1999 (with a two-year break in the 1970s), hosted by Daryl Somers. Nearing the end of its run when *The Castle* was released in 1997, *Hey Hey* was famous (or infamous) for its low-budget and ramshackle format, with a style of humour that was becoming increasingly outdated and corny.

GENRE, STRUCTURE & LANGUAGE

Comedy

The Castle is a classic underdog comedy: the characters that the audience is encouraged to identify with – the Kerrigan family and their neighbours – come from positions of little or no power and have to fight back against a much more powerful adversary, in this case the Barlow Group and its legal representatives. Part of the joy in the film is seeing Darryl initially refuse to accept the decisions of a higher authority or conform to the established ways of opposing them, and then how he is able to 'play by the rules' and still come out triumphant.

A core element of the style of the comedy is observational humour: the film identifies aspects of Australian suburban life that audiences recognise as true to their own experiences. Often it is not even necessary to make a joke since simply recognising an attitude or behaviour represented on screen can be enough to make people laugh. An example of this is the exchange in the kitchen between Darryl and Steve about the various cars that need to be moved so that Darryl can get to the car that he wants. This was one of the scenes used in the original advertising campaign for the film as it captures a very recognisable scenario of a family with more cars than they need (some possibly not even roadworthy), resulting in constant negotiation about moving them around. The humour is in the familiarity and absurdity of the situation rather than from an actual punchline. *The Castle* often exaggerates aspects of Australian suburban culture, but it always remains grounded enough in reality to be funny. This style of social parody through slight embellishment is characteristic of the humour throughout the film.

The humour in *The Castle* also relies heavily on recurring gags that become funnier the more they appear, just as stand-up comics might use call-backs to reference previous jokes in their routine. Rather than tiring of the jokes, the audience increasingly enjoys them.

Some of the recurring jokes in *The Castle* include:

- the constant sound of aeroplanes landing and taking off, with Darryl reiterating how happy he is to live next to the airport
- Sal's kitsch and tacky handicraft work
- Steve and Darryl discussing items for sale in *The Trading Post*
- Darryl's admiration of Sal's basic cooking
- Darryl declaring that items he values are going 'straight to the pool room'
- Darryl's references to the serenity at Bonnie Doon.

Courtroom drama

The Castle also incorporates aspects of a courtroom, or legal, drama, as the film's main source of conflict and its resolution play out at the Administrative Appeals Tribunal, the Federal Court and the High Court. Typical of courtroom dramas, during these scenes issues of morality, law and justice are explored, and the drama (or humour) is generated by the conflict between the two sides and the question of which side can present the most persuasive argument and ultimately win the case. The scenes where Darryl is represented by Dennis are played for laughs, as it is clear that there is no chance they will win; but the climactic scene in which Darryl is represented by Lawrence generates real tension, as not only is it Darryl's last hope of keeping his house, but this time he really has a chance of winning.

Structure

The narrative structure of *The Castle* is linear: the events happen in chronological order, although with substantial use of flashbacks. For example, the opening montage in which Dale introduces family members almost entirely comprises flashbacks as Dale gives us key pieces of information about the family. In fact, arguably the entire film is one big flashback as Dale is narrating events that occurred in his past.

The film is traditionally structured: it begins by introducing the characters and setting; it then introduces a source of conflict (the house being compulsorily acquired); this provides the characters with motivation (their desire to prevent the acquisition); the characters encounter various obstacles and setbacks (losing appeals); and then, in the climax, they are ultimately triumphant at the High Court. The episode of the first trip to Bonnie Doon has no real narrative purpose, other than helping to further establish characters and provide humour, but Dale's reference near the end of the film to Lawrence's regular visits there helps to provide a strong sense of closure.

Use of a narrator

While the overall style of *The Castle* is naturalistic (see 'Cinematography', page 16), the very first and final shots are not. They show Dale Kerrigan against a black background, shot in a medium close-up and speaking directly to the audience. This is a way of introducing him at the start of the film as its narrator, and reminding us at the end that the film is a story he is telling. These shots do briefly break from the realism of the film, but not in a way that significantly disrupts the audience's ability to invest emotionally in the storytelling or to believe in the internal logic of the film.

Using Dale as the narrator serves a few purposes, including allowing him to move the story along, provide background information on characters and events that are not otherwise depicted, and to help with the transitions between scenes. However, his narration is also often apparently redundant as he literally describes what is shown on screen or tells us a character says something right before the character says exactly this line. This might be considered poor filmmaking as it is 'telling rather than showing' and duplicating the information delivered to the audience, but in the case of *The Castle* it reinforces Dale's sweet and arguably simple nature which makes him feel the need to constantly spell out everything. His deadpan stating of the obvious also functions comedically when what he describes completely conflicts with what is shown on screen – for instance, after we see Dale and Wayne facing each other in silence or conversing in monosyllables, the narration says 'we get on great; we can just chat for hours' (06:42).

Possibly the most important thing to note about Dale's narration is that, as a supporting character who is involved in the action during the film, his perspective – and therefore the perspective of the film – is completely subjective: events and characters are presented to the audience in the way that Dale feels about them. Seeing the world through his eyes is a significant factor in the film's feelgood tone, and it also provides much of the humour when the audience is one step ahead of Dale, recognising the reality of a situation that the somewhat naive Dale cannot see.

Cinematography

The Castle uses very conventional cinematography. Most scenes are shot in a way that does not draw attention to the fact that it is a filmed work of fiction, so it is received by the audience as naturalistic. The washed out and dull colours give the film an unglamorous and overcast look that emphasises the ordinariness of the world these characters live in, as opposed to the glossy and rich visuals of the average big-budget Hollywood film.

The camera is mostly kept at a very comfortable distance from the characters; it functionally follows the action and dialogue and ensures the audience members are not overly conscious of the fact they are watching a film. Most of the shots that include two or more characters are medium shots, and medium close-ups are used for a single character. Both types of shot provide a natural balance between the background and the subjects in the foreground. Some medium long shots are used, which show more background, such as the scene when Darryl is showing John Clifton around his house. Long shots are also used to show the exteriors of houses and other buildings; these can be described as establishing shots as their purpose is to introduce the setting of specific scenes. Towards the end, when the filmmakers particularly want the characters' words to resonate with the audience, there are close-ups of Darryl and Lawrence – the whole face of the character fills the screen – as they deliver key speeches.

Editing

Montage sequences – numerous shots from many different points in the plot, edited together – are often used to convey the passing of time; more significantly, they are used at the start of the film to introduce all the characters and at the end to let the audience know what happened to them next. *The Castle* also uses dissolves – where one shot briefly overlaps with the next – to indicate the passing of a short period of time, sometimes even within one scene. To indicate longer periods of time passing, fade-outs and fade-ins are used: the shot dissolves to a black screen which then dissolves into the next scene.

SCENE-BY-SCENE ANALYSIS

The divisions below follow the chapters in the DVD version of *The Castle*. Note that time codes can vary from player to player, but those referenced in this guide should be close enough for you to locate a particular scene or quote.

Chapter 1: A happy home (0:00:00)

Summary: *Dale Kerrigan introduces his family and conveys how much they all love their home, especially his father, Darryl Kerrigan.*

During the opening credits there are the sounds of birds chirping, a lawnmower and a dog barking: all iconic Australian suburban sounds. The film then fades into a formally framed medium close-up shot of Dale Kerrigan who faces the camera, introduces himself and establishes himself as the narrator of the film. The next shot is an establishing shot of the house at 3 Highview Crescent, Coolaroo, the film's primary setting and its source of drama, as it will soon be revealed that the house is under threat.

Darryl appears on screen for the first time, in a conventional medium close-up, as Dale's narration continues to tell us how happy Darryl is to live there, even though many of the details Dale describes about the house and its location are things most people would consider undesirable – such as the nearby power pylons, which Darryl sees as 'a reminder of man's ability to generate electricity' (0:1:26). This sets up the main recurring joke about the Kerrigans being happy to live next to an airport, which also reveals how the family always see positives where others see negatives, and provides some insight into their socioeconomic status.

Dale's monologue continues over a montage of shots of the other family members, whom he introduces, also discussing how close and caring they all are. He then tells us about the family pets, four greyhounds, another detail that suggests the family's working-class identity. The next sequence shows Darryl receiving Father's Day gifts, which establishes the fondness between the family members who take pleasure in making, giving and receiving small gifts as they cannot afford anything grander. This sequence also establishes the running joke about Darryl enshrining the things he considers to be 'special' in the pool room.

Q Thinking about how the Kerrigan family are introduced in this scene, to what extent does the film seem to be laughing at them and to what extent does it encourage us to find them endearing? How much does this change over the course of the film?

Chapter 2: Property evaluation (0:08:50)

Summary: *John Clifton does an evaluation of the land and property at 3 Highview Crescent on behalf of the council.*

John Clifton, from the local council, visits to do an evaluation of the Kerrigans' property, which facilitates humour about Darryl being naive and borderline delusional about how much his house is worth. A shot of the runway, with the planes in the background, the cyclone fence in the middle ground and the twigs of a tree branch in the foreground, reinforces how close the property is to the airport. The sound of squelching mud is heard as the men walk around the yard, again establishing the less-than-ideal condition of the property. Darryl also reveals that one area of the backyard is landfill and that testing revealed there is 'nothing too serious' (0:11:42) in the ground, although he then asks about lead, which is an extremely toxic substance. Later in the day the Kerrigans are at the dinner table and Dale is worried that Darryl is considering selling as a result of the evaluation, but Darryl assures him that he is simply keen to find out what the house is worth.

Key point

Until now, the audience has only seen the rest of the family's reaction to Darryl and his pride in his home, which, of course, is out of step with how most people would respond to his enthusiasm. John is the first person in the film to present the perspective of an outsider, and his bewildered facial expressions convey the likely reactions of most audience members to Darryl's point of view up to this point in the story.

Q How is John Clifton presented to the audience? Is he identifiable and endearing, or menacing and a threat? Considering he is part of the system that will attempt to take away Darryl's home, why is he presented in this way?

Chapter 3: Compulsory acquisition (0:12:40)

Summary: *The Kerrigans discover that their and their neighbours' houses will be compulsorily acquired, which is confirmed by Darryl's unsuccessful visit to the municipal offices and the advice from his lawyer, Dennis Denuto.*

Darryl, Sal and Dale read the letter informing them that their house is being compulsorily acquired (forcibly bought by the government). They are in a state of shocked disbelief. They discover their neighbours Farouk and Jack are also being forced to leave. The next scene begins with an establishing shot of the local municipal offices, followed by Darryl having a meeting with a councillor who confirms the airport is expanding and needs more space, and therefore Darryl's home is being compulsorily acquired. Darryl does not want the compensation on offer; he simply does not want to move. This scene reflects both sides of the debate: on one side is the airport, which has a legally binding agreement with all levels of government that allows it to take the land it needs, and on the other side is Darryl, who does not recognise that agreement, as it does not take him into account.

We then see Darryl untying his greyhounds outside the municipal offices and walking down the street with them, set to a melancholic song, presenting him as a troubled man. This shot then fades to a shot of Darryl walking down a busy suburban street and going into a run-down building; the camera pans to the window of his solicitor's unimpressive office above a shop. A sound bridge of Dennis Denuto talking to Darryl helps provide the transition to the scene inside the lawyer's office, where Dennis is trying to explain that he does not have the qualifications or experience to help Darryl with his case. The situation is both funny and endearing as it is obvious that Dennis is not suitable for the job, but Darryl still has faith in him.

Q To what extent does the film present Darryl's argument – that the agreement allowing the airport to acquire his land might be legal, but should not apply to him as he was never part of the discussion – as a reasonable stance?

Chapter 4: Dinner, stories & telly (0:17:29)

Summary: *It is life as usual for the Kerrigans who believe that, with Dennis' help, everything will be okay.*

The Kerrigans enjoy a trouble-free dinner and then settle down together to enjoy the ritual of watching *Hey Hey It's Saturday*. The moment is slightly bittersweet as Dale cannot help but think of Wayne in prison. Wayne is seen lying on his prison bed, looking up at a family photo on his cell wall. A fade-out followed by a fade-in indicates that it is now a new day. Darryl is excitedly talking to Dennis, believing everything will be okay. Darryl praises Sal's new piece of handicraft and there is an instance of Darryl's catchphrase 'tell him he's dreaming', in response to the price of an item Steve has found in *The Trading Post*. Darryl announces a trip to Bonnie Doon and the scene ends with him saying he will give their neighbours the news that everything will be alright.

Q What are the recurring jokes that appear in this scene and how are they used to suggest that life is now back to normal for the Kerrigan family?

Chapter 5: Trace & Con's holiday (0:20:46)

Summary: *Tracey and Con return home from their honeymoon.*

Upbeat music accompanies an establishing shot of the international arrival terminal at the airport where the Kerrigans have gone to greet Tracey and Con, who have just arrived home from their honeymoon in Thailand. A series of long shots and medium long shots shows everybody walking home together from the airport to the house, once more reinforcing the gag about them living so close to the airport. Back home Con and Tracey describe their experience on the plane, enthusing about details such as free sleep masks, the food, the films on offer and the music channels. The humour in this scene comes from how impressed the couple, and the rest of the family, are by the everyday aspects of plane travel, which is a reflection of how uncommon air travel used to be for ordinary families, especially working-class ones.

The scene dissolves to a later point in the conversation. Tracey and Con are giving out presents: they are all typical tourist items (including a fake Rolex watch). The family members are all very impressed by their gifts, prompting Darryl to repeat the 'going straight to the pool room' punchline. In the next scene, Dale once more visits Wayne in prison, and we see Wayne smile for the first time when he receives his gift of a carved elephant. The slightly melancholic end to the scene involves Dale avoiding telling Wayne they are all going to Bonnie Doon, knowing how much Wayne loves going there.

Q When the characters show how impressed they are by the mundane aspects of air travel, do you think the film is positioning the audience to laugh *at* the characters, or *with* them? Explain your answer.

Chapter 6: Goin' to Bonnie Doon (0:23:34)

Summary: *The Kerrigans go to their holiday home in Bonnie Doon.*

The scene begins in the car driving to Bonnie Doon, with Darryl singing his annoyingly repetitive song. When the scene cuts to the family unloading the car, Dale, as the narrator, discusses how wonderful Bonnie Doon is, which comedically contrasts with shots of the landscape looking overcast and dreary, with huge pylons dominating the scene. Similarly to the family home in Coolaroo, the holiday house at Bonnie Doon is depicted as being undesirable to most people, which makes Darryl's love for it funny but also touching, reiterating that he has the ability to see the best in everything. In this scene we first hear Darryl praising the 'serenity' of Bonnie Doon, which also becomes a recurring joke.

There is a fade-out and fade-in to the next day and we see Darryl, Dale and Steve on the boat, the joke being that, while Darryl loves 'serenity', he also loves the very noisy boat. Back at the holiday house Tracey is giving Sal a hair treatment while they discuss when Tracey will have kids, a rare moment between the only two major female characters in the film. During the conversation it is clear that Sal is hiding her concern about the upcoming court hearing about the acquisition.

Q Up until this point the film has not focused much on Sal or Tracey, other than in relation to the male characters. How does the scene between just the two of them present them in a different light?

Chapter 7: How's the serenity? (0:28:20)

Summary: *The Kerrigans enjoy being at Bonnie Doon.*

Con practises his kickboxing and Tracey attempts to hold the punching bag for him, which is comedic but also endearing as, despite their superficial differences, it shows they are a loving couple. Darryl and Sal look on admiringly at Con's discipline and passion, and Darryl comments on the serenity, while in the background we can hear Steve's motorcycle. There is then a humorous montage consisting of various shots of Darryl and Sal kissing and embracing, dissolving back and forth with various shots of the bleak landscape of Bonnie Doon, accompanied by a romantic song on the soundtrack. The sequence is a parody of the picturesque and romantic montages of conventional cinema. The montage cuts to dinnertime with Darryl handing out pieces of charred steak, suggesting they may be underdone: another joke about the family's simple, unpretentious tastes. There is more humour in the continued discussion of Tracey and Con's honeymoon in Thailand, which Darryl cannot imagine being better than Bonnie Doon.

Q Thinking about the way romantic love is usually presented in film and television, which established film conventions are being spoofed in this scene? Does this make the couples in *The Castle* appear ridiculous or perhaps more sincere?

Chapter 8: The appeal (0:32:00)

Summary: *Darryl loses his appeal against the acquisition and decides to take legal action.*

A slow fade-out and fade-in are used to signify a slightly longer passage of time. It is now Monday morning and Darryl is ready for, and feeling optimistic about, the appeal. The scene cuts to the Administrative Appeals Tribunal building and then to the interior where Darryl is at the hearing. The room is almost empty, with apparently only Farouk sitting behind Darryl in support. The Administrative Appeals Tribunal chairperson presses Darryl about the legal grounds for his argument and asserts it is up to Darryl to demonstrate why his house cannot be acquired since it is legally authorised. Darryl is incredulous that somebody can simply take his house away and gives a spirited defence of his position. The film cuts to a later scene where he, Sal, Farouk and Jack are sitting around the table; it is confirmed that he lost the appeal, which is no surprise to the audience, who are aware that, from a legal perspective, Darryl's arguments were tenuous. The others commiserate with Darryl, but he decides to keep fighting and to enlist a lawyer.

Q To what extent is the audience made to feel one step ahead of Darryl at this point of the film? How does his surprise at losing the appeal endear Darryl to the audience?

Chapter 9: The big artillery (0:36:15)

Summary: *Darryl convinces Dennis to represent him in court.*

The film cuts to an establishing exterior shot of Dennis' dilapidated office building and then to inside the office, where Darryl is standing next to Dennis, who is swearing at the photocopier. Once composed, Dennis tells Darryl that nobody he knows wants to represent Darryl against the Barlow Group, the airport's major investor. Darryl persists in arguing that Dennis should handle the case, demonstrating that he has more faith in Dennis than Dennis has in himself.

The next scene is an affectionate one between Darryl and Tracey as they sit on the couch, talking and watching television. Despite all Darryl's worries, he does not let his concern show while with Tracey. When Dale sees Darryl and Tracey laughing on the sofa, his narration shows this is another moment when the family having fun triggers his awareness that Wayne is missing out, making this scene a reminder of the highs and lows that the Kerrigan family have gone through before.

The film fades to a shot of Dennis' office, with a music sound bridge aiding the transition, to indicate that the scenes inside the Kerrigan home, Wayne's prison cell and Dennis' office are all happening at the same time. Dennis is shown dictating a legal letter about Darryl's case into a tape recorder, and then listening back to the recorder to type out the letter himself on a typewriter. This funny moment reminds the audience that Dennis' legal practice is so small-time he does not always have an assistant available to type his dictation, but it also reveals that Dennis is now committed to representing Darryl.

Key point

This scene effectively presents Darryl's principled stance against the acquisition: no matter how big and powerful the Barlow Group is, it still has to play by the rules, and right will win over wrong. Darryl's enthusiasm and optimism is so persuasive that, despite his cynicism, pessimism and feeling of inadequacy, Dennis is convinced to help Darryl with the case.

Q What does it say about Dennis' character that he agrees to represent Darryl despite his severe reservations? What does it say about Darryl's character that he is so persuasive?

Chapter 10: Threats (0:40:42)

Summary: *The Barlow Group's solicitor, Rob Graham, meets with Dennis and offers a new compensation deal, which Darryl turns down.*

Establishing shots of the city are followed by a close-up of a hand sorting through mail addressed to 'Hammersley & Laycock, Barrister & Solicitor', including a letter from Dennis Denuto's office. This is an effective way of showing the audience that Dennis has filed his legal challenge against a large and prestigious law firm. Then the film cuts back to the Kerrigan house, where numerous things are going wrong: this day is not going well for Darryl.

Next there is a shot of lawyer Ron Graham looking for Dennis' office, and smirking when he spots the solicitor's sign on the upstairs window of a dilapidated building. Ron clearly thinks – correctly – that Dennis is a small-time solicitor. Ron and Dennis discuss Darryl's case; Ron makes a new offer, Dennis doubts Darryl will accept it and Ron delivers a thinly veiled warning about what might happen as a result. The film cuts to Darryl on the phone defiantly refusing the offer, once more proving himself to be fearless and righteous.

Q How does this scene represent the power or status imbalance between Ron and Dennis?

Chapter 11: Passin' on messages (0:44:25)

Summary: *Sal tells the story about meeting Darryl and realising he was a man of principles. A man comes to the house to threaten Darryl, one of their cars is vandalised, and Darryl and Steve retaliate.*

An establishing shot of the front of the Kerrigans' house in the evening is followed by a shot inside where the family are having dessert. Darryl is clearly unhappy and distracted, going through the 'what do you call this?' routine without the usual enthusiasm. In a rare moment of doubt, he asks if turning the money down was the right thing to do. Sal assures him it was, although Steve is not so sure. Sal then tells the story of when Darryl and she first met: Darryl left her alone when he realised she was on a date with somebody else. The story demonstrates to Steve and the rest of the family that Darryl is a man of principles and that is why he could never accept the money.

There is a knock at the door and Darryl goes to answer it. The man at the door – dressed all in black, with a leather jacket, gold chain and large moustache – looks threatening. Darryl is initially calm until it is clear that the man is threatening him and then Darryl loses his cool. Steve chases the man away by brandishing a gun.

Later that night Darryl rushes out of bed to discover the windscreen of Steve's car has been smashed. The scene then cuts to Darryl and Steve in their tow truck driving off in the dark, then to the pair yelling into the intercom at the gates of a large property, before cutting to a sequence in which they attach chains to the wrought-iron gates and drive off, dragging the gates behind them. The sequence is comedically set to music that evokes a spy or heist film.

The next morning Sergeant Mick Kennedy knocks on Darryl's door to question him about the missing gates. Mick knows exactly what Darryl has done, but decides to turn a blind eye. The punchline of the scene is Mick telling Darryl to put the gates at the back of the house – the joke being that they have been left in plain sight, out the front. Darryl is clearly not good at either theft or lying, which makes him all the more endearing to Mick and the audience.

Key point

This scene contains one of the film's most overt statements about class differences. The contrast between where the Kerrigans live and the house Darryl and Steve visit in this scene is significant, as they are now clearly in a much more affluent neighbourhood characterised by wide tree-lined streets and large houses with high fences. Later the suburb is identified as Toorak, which is one of Melbourne's most affluent suburbs.

Q Are Darryl and Steve's actions in this scene justified?

Chapter 12: The Constitution (0:50:13)

Summary: *The Federal Court case begins, in which Dennis invokes the Constitution and Mabo.*

Darryl holds a meeting in his shed with Steve and his neighbours Farouk, Jack and Evonne (who has been mentioned once before, but we only see for the first time now). They discuss the threats they have received and give Darryl their support. When they discuss the fees for legally challenging the Barlow Group, Darryl once more proves what a noble person he is by declaring he will cover Jack's share of the costs, as he knows Jack cannot afford it. Darryl expresses his confidence in Dennis and the film then comedically cuts to a shot of Darryl and Dennis in the Federal Court, with Dennis clearly out of his depth, shuffling through papers and nervously stalling for time. A shot of the defendant's lawyer, Ron Graham, shows him looking calm, confident and bemused at Dennis' awkwardness. Dennis claims that what is happening to Darryl is in violation of the Constitution and he invokes the Mabo case of 1992. Ron displays his confidence and arrogance, barely able to stifle his laughter, and does not bother to argue the case in response.

Q While Dennis is clearly a figure of ridicule in this scene, how do later events in the film vindicate him?

Chapter 13: A chance meeting (0:56:16)

Summary: *Darryl meets Lawrence; Darryl loses the court case.*

Outside the court building upbeat music matches Darryl's optimistic mood. When he walks back into the courtroom building, he meets Lawrence Hammill. Most of their initial interaction is suffused with humour arising from Darryl assuming 'Laurie' has a similar background and set of experiences to him. An early indication that Lawrence is a kind and accepting person is that he is not offended, nor does he say anything to embarrass Darryl. Instead, the two men enjoy their mutual pride in their children – something not defined by social class – and a bond is formed. Darryl returns to the courtroom and the judge delivers the verdict in favour of the Barlow Group. Back at the house Darryl is devastated, bewildered and exhausted.

Q How does the film present Lawrence in this scene? What are the clues that he and his situation are not as Darryl assumes?

Chapter 14: Out in two weeks (0:59:53)

Summary: *Darryl is devastated and the family prepare to move out of the house.*

During dinner Darryl grimly delivers the news that they have to move out in two weeks and melancholic music accompanies shots of the various family members looking upset. The extent to which Darryl is broken by the outcome is noticed by other family members who observe he is not behaving like himself, neither engaging in the routine of complimenting Sal's cooking nor losing his temper at the injustice. He is simply defeated.

After a scene at Pentridge jail where Wayne hears the news from Dale, the film cuts back to the pool room where Darryl is packing up his most beloved objects. A close-up pan of the various pool room treasures now gives those items more poignancy than before: while the audience would previously have laughed at them for being kitsch and tacky, they now appreciate the true value of these items to Darryl. Steve then enters and does something that Kerrigan men often have trouble doing: he tells his father how he feels about him. Neither father nor son say any more after that and Steve leaves, but it is a rare and touching moment in which Steve expresses his admiration and love for Darryl, who is more used to giving out compliments than receiving them. Sal then enters; they discuss helping Jack, and Darryl makes a comparison between the situation they are facing and what happened to First Nations Australians when their land was stolen from them, a sentiment that is well-intended if somewhat naive, especially by contemporary standards. The moment is interrupted by Steve popping back in with Lawrence, who has come to see Darryl.

Key point

While many of the recurring jokes in the film are played just for laughs, this scene is a good example of how these jokes (or lack of them) are used to convey character information. So much of Darryl's personality is demonstrated by his ability to see the positive side of everything and through his almost tunnel-vision love for his family, which is the underlying source of humour for so many of the recurring gags. So it really is significant that he is now so defeated he can no longer bring himself to praise Sal's cooking as he usually would.

Q Is Darryl right to compare his situation to that of First Nations Australians? By doing this, does the film trivialise the experiences of First Nations Australians or does it help bring awareness to broader audiences?

Chapter 15: Laurie takes the reins (1:05:30)

Summary: *Lawrence offers to represent Darryl and a new case in the High Court begins.*

Lawrence reveals that he is a retired Queen's Counsel and believes Darryl does actually have a case in law. When Darryl then queries how the case can go any further the film cuts to a low-angle shot of Dennis, Darryl and Lawrence standing outside the High Court in Canberra, three weeks later. Positioning the camera slightly below the trio gives them a heroic appearance, which is accompanied by military-style marching music to give the moment a sense of importance and occasion. Inside the courtroom the 'call-to-arms' style of music continues and a series of dissolves captures the seriousness and prestige of the proceedings.

When Lawrence addresses the court, he is filmed in medium close-up so he dominates the screen. He speaks directly and articulately, and makes a compelling argument; this is a complete contrast to Dennis' earlier well-meaning but bumbling court appearance. It is also in contrast to the team of five lawyers on the other side, who are shot together in a single frame, with one addressing the court while the others confer in the background. The contrast between the two teams reinforces the 'David versus Goliath' nature of the entire situation, with Lawrence representing the underdogs (Darryl and his neighbours) and the opposing lawyer, Mr Lyle, representing the powerful Barlow Group. The scene continues as a series of dissolve shots to create a montage of the two very skilful lawyers challenging each other's arguments, even getting philosophical. However, the civility of the proceedings comes to an end when Mr Lyle enrages Darryl by suggesting Wayne is in jail because of the type of house he grew up in.

Q While many earlier parts of the film encourage us to laugh at Darryl and his family, why is it that, in this scene, we are now encouraged to share his outrage at Mr Lyle's arrogance and disdain?

Chapter 16: It's a home (1:11:59)

Summary: *Outside the courtroom Darryl delivers a passionate monologue about the value of a home, which inspires Lawrence's summing-up speech to the court, helping them to win the case.*

Outside the courthouse Dennis, Lawrence and Darryl stand in the wind in a medium shot, staring into the distance. After saying that he wishes he had Lawrence's words, clearly appreciating the power of education and rhetoric, Darryl delivers the most important speech of the film in which he articulates its main theme: a home is more than just a house, and you cannot put a price on the shared memories and experiences that make a home so special. This speech reveals that Darryl is aware that his house is not very impressive, despite all his claims throughout the film, and the audience realises that his pride in the additions he has made to the house is due purely to the fact that he and his family built them.

The film cuts back to inside the court with a close-up of Lawrence, whose face fills the screen as he delivers his final statement about how the Constitution does apply to this case. Afterwards there is a dissolve to the judges giving their outcome and it is revealed that Darryl has won.

Key point

In his narration, Dale tells us that Darryl had a real moment of pride when he realised Lawrence was quoting him. The close-up of Darryl's smiling face as he listens to Lawrence is moving and endearing, as this is the moment when Darryl realises that not only does he have the intelligence and ability to express himself in a meaningful way, but his use of rhetoric is so effective that even an experienced QC like Lawrence has taken inspiration from him.

Q Despite all his blundering, does this scene vindicate Dennis in any way?

Q Why does Lawrence feel this was his most satisfying victory in forty years?

Chapter 17: Life after court (1:16:14)

Summary: *The Kerrigans celebrate and everybody goes on to have happy lives.*

There is a big party at the Kerrigans' home for family, neighbours and friends. Lawrence brings his son Adam with him, which demonstrates the friendship across class divides that is growing between him and Darryl. The love between Darryl and Sal is as strong as ever, demonstrated by shots of them smiling at each other across the room from different conversation groups in the party.

The final moments of the film mirror the opening sequence as it is another montage of the various characters accompanied by Dale's narration, but this time he is telling the audience what happened to everybody after the court case. Wayne is released from jail with Lawrence's help; Dennis achieves professional success, pursuing a class action against those who dumped lead in landfill; Lawrence and Darryl go fishing together at Bonnie Doon and become good friends; Steve gets married and has a son; Con and Tracey also have a son; Wayne joins, and expands, Darryl's tow-truck business; Sal takes up pottery; and Darryl finishes the patio and extensions, installs the iron gates and is content with life. The montage ends with a shot of a plane going overhead, and a close-up of Dale smiling at the camera, saying 'My name's Dale Kerrigan and that was my story' (1:19:19).

Chapter 18: End credits (1:19:27)

There is a final shot of the family photo and then the screen fades to black. The credits roll, accompanied by 'We've Only Just Begun' sung by Kate Ceberano, implying that this is not the end of the Kerrigans' story, but with new relationships, new friendships, new children, a growing business and new extensions to the house, their lives are just beginning a new phase.

CHARACTERS & RELATIONSHIPS

Darryl Kerrigan

Key quotes

'Dad is the backbone of the Kerrigan family.' (Dale, 0:01:33)

'Dad also had a way of makin' everyone feel important.' (Dale, 0:17:38)

'It is right and fair that a family be allowed to live in its own house.' (Darryl, 0:34:25)

Darryl is the driving force behind the Kerrigan family and the film's protagonist, whose relentless optimism and love for his family and home is reflected in everything he does. He sees positives where other people see negatives, which is encapsulated in his belief that living next to an airport is a good thing. He takes considerable pride in his home-improvement projects, and his joy comes more from the fact that he does these things himself rather than whether or not they are successful. Darryl adores his family, especially his wife Sal, and two of the main running jokes throughout the film are based on the disproportionate delight and enjoyment he gets from her handicrafts and her cooking. The pleasure Darryl takes in the most mundane things Sal does makes these repeated gags quite touching.

The way Darryl dresses indicates his social and economic class. When he shows John Clifton around his property, Darryl is wearing large ugg boots, which used to be considered a defining accessory of the Australian 'bogan', along with faded jeans and flannel shirts, both of which Darryl also wears. Later in the film when Darryl decides to face the authorities to challenge the acquisition of his house, he starts wearing more muted clothes, such as a blue shirt with a brown jumper, in order to allow the audience to take him more seriously. Later again, he wears a suit, to demonstrate how serious he is about his court appearances.

Darryl is a tow-truck driver, which at the time of the film's release would have established him as a working-class, blue-collar worker who would not have a high income. Nevertheless, he owns his own truck, and built the holiday house at Bonnie Doon from a kit. These details demonstrate that he is a self-made person who can provide for his family, and he is shown to take pride in his work. Despite this, Darryl thinks that what he has is due to luck, which also suggests humility.

His instinctive mistrust of authority is first evident when John Clifton arrives and Darryl defensively assumes that the visit is because he has broken council regulations. However, he does admire and respect expertise, even though his judgement is not always sound. Part of what makes Darryl such a likeable character is his encouragement and support of others, praising Sal for making a basic meal or an ugly piece of pottery, or putting faith in Dennis, despite it being clear that Dennis is not qualified for the job. Even though Dennis unsuccessfully represented Wayne in court, Darryl still praises him for having done his best.

Darryl displays some attitudes that, while not overtly racist, are perhaps racially insensitive, such as the speech he makes at Tracey and Con's wedding, applying Greek stereotypes to the groom and his parents. On the other hand, he completely welcomes Con into his family, and he also embraces Farouk, who is Lebanese, as a friend and neighbour. It is telling that Darryl immediately agrees to Farouk's request to help him with reading a letter, without any judgement or sense of superiority.

Darryl also embodies the old-fashioned trait associated with masculinity, of not revealing his true emotions, especially when he is feeling sad or despondent. Rather than inferring that he is emotionally repressed, it could be argued that his tendency to hide the fact that he is upset is more due to him wanting to project a cheery persona, to reassure his family and others that everything is going to be alright. The first indication that Darryl hides his true feelings is when Dennis asks after Wayne: Darryl briefly looks heartbroken, before quickly switching back to his happy-go-lucky persona and saying that Wayne is fine. It is a moment that captures the extent to which Darryl puts on a brave face when dealing with adversity and adopts an easygoing and optimistic approach, when he really does have hidden pain. Another example of how much Darryl cares for his family and takes responsibility for looking after them is during the holiday to Bonnie Doon, when he says he wishes Wayne was with them and that he could have done better by him. Similarly, Darryl blames himself when the court hearings do not go to plan, further displaying his humility and how much of the family's burden he takes upon himself.

Darryl is distinguished by his strong principles, demonstrated by him constantly refusing all offers of monetary compensation in exchange for leaving the house he loves, and by the tale of when he first met Sal, leaving her alone after discovering she already had a boyfriend. He is also instinctively generous, paying Jack's share of the legal fees and offering him a place to stay.

Key point

Darryl is able to see people for who they are, and to form friendships that transcend social divisions such as class differences. This is apparent in the ease with which he approaches Lawrence and later befriends him. Not being intimidated by or hostile towards people from more privileged backgrounds or different socioeconomic classes is another sign of Darryl's good character and is in keeping with Australians' image of themselves as egalitarian. Lawrence, to his credit, takes Darryl in his stride, too, and is not intimidated by or dismissive of him either. The friendship between these two men is very significant, reflecting Australians' belief that they are less constrained by social divisions than people in other countries.

Sal Kerrigan

Key quotes

'If Dad is the backbone, Mum is the other bones, all of 'em. She keeps the family together.' (Dale, 0:02:11)

'And that's what I love about him: his principles.' (Sal, talking about Darryl, 0:46:25)

Darryl's wife and the mother of their four children, Sal is a traditional housewife who runs the household and prepares the meals. At the start of the film Dale tells us that Sal also has a part-time job, further emphasising her ability to balance numerous roles and responsibilities. Sal is often the voice of reason, subtly calming Darryl when he gets carried away, and nurturing him when the severity of the situation overwhelms him. She loves Darryl and her children unreservedly, and takes pride in looking after them.

Sal's story about first meeting Darryl reflects what are now somewhat outdated attitudes about chivalry: Darryl is seen as being noble for not 'cutting another man's lunch', which is slang for attempting to romance a woman who is already dating another man. Perhaps in an updated version of this story the principled Darryl would leave Sal alone simply because she had made it clear she was not interested. Sal is also portrayed as quietly wise, deeply compassionate and, most of all, able to see through Darryl's bravado when nobody else can.

Dale Kerrigan

Key quotes

'My name is Dale Kerrigan, and this is my story.' (Dale, 0:00:44)

'Our family is very close knit.' (Dale, 0:06:47)

The youngest of the four Kerrigan children, Dale is sweet-natured, artless and sensitive; he adores his family, especially Darryl, whom he idolises. His innocent acceptance of things at face value provides much of the ironic humour in the film. Seeing his family happy and together is very important to Dale. The film reminds us of this every time Dale happily observes things such as affection between his parents or family members laughing together. Dale is also deeply empathetic, especially towards his brother Wayne. Whenever Dale is enjoying himself, especially with the family, he immediately feels sad that Wayne is not also sharing the joy. Dale misses his brother deeply and, unlike the other men in the Kerrigan family, does not attempt to hide his feelings – at least, as far as the audience is concerned.

Steve Kerrigan

Key quote

'Dad, you haven't let anyone down. I don't know what the opposite of lettin' someone down is, but you done the opposite.' (Steve, 1:03:01)

Along with Dale, Steve is the other one of the four adult Kerrigan offspring who still lives at home with Darryl and Sal. He is an apprentice mechanic who loves buying and trading through *The Trading Post,* often bonding with Darryl over their amusement about and disdain for people who put too high a price on the things they are trying to sell. Steve is also expert at knocking those prices down, and is proud of his reputation for being a good negotiator: he is thrilled when Con praises his haggling ability. He is also an 'ideas man', as Darryl says (0:03:24), and is constantly impressing Darryl with his inventions, such as a combined brush and hose. Although not as obviously expressive as some other family members, and the one most prone to losing his temper, Steve is just as caring and sincere. He is also fiercely protective of Darryl, which is evident when he threatens the man at the door with a gun.

Tracey Kerrigan

Key quote

'She is the only member of the Kerrigan family who'd had a tertiary education.' (Dale, 0:04:15)

Tracey is Darryl's favourite child because she has had a tertiary education, in the form of a certificate in hairdressing. Tracey is very much in love with her new husband Con, but also remains close to her family. She wants to focus on her career before settling down to raise a family of her own. She is able to tell when either of her parents is worried or upset, despite their efforts to hide their feelings. While considered to be the most glamorous member of the family, Tracey is often shown wearing tight acid-wash jeans and ugly jumpers, and her hair is permed, all of which were popular in the 1980s and 1990s and combine to create a stereotypical look strongly associated with working-class suburban culture.

Wayne Kerrigan

Key quotes

'Wayne always reckoned he was doin' fine but, I get the feelin' he was missin' us more than he was lettin' on.' (Dale, 0:19:03)

'The only reason I love that house is 'cause it had him and mum in it.' (Wayne, 1:01:34)

The eldest brother in the Kerrigan family, Wayne is doing an eight-year prison sentence for armed robbery. He is often shown to be expressionless and still; however, rather than this being menacing, he appears to be a simple soul who yearns to return home, often lying on his bed gazing wistfully at the family photo on his cell wall. He adores Darryl and has complete faith in his ability to make sure the family do not lose the house. The exchange between Wayne and Dale in which Wayne asks how everybody is and Dale simply says 'good' each time is a funny observation on how men, particularly brothers, are not necessarily good communicators, but at the same time it conveys the fact that the pair do care about each other and the rest of the family, and do not need to put their feelings into words. Like Darryl and Steve, Wayne puts on a brave face to make sure the others don't see how vulnerable he is.

Key point

When Dale tells us how much the family still love Wayne, it serves three purposes. It establishes that the Kerrigans have experienced pain despite their optimistic outlook; it reminds the audience that the Kerrigans belong to a social class more prone to being involved in criminal activity; and it reinforces the loving nature of the family as they all still care for Wayne despite what he has done.

Con Petropoulous

Key quote

'This case has totally regained my faith in the legal system.' (Con, 1:16:23)

An accountant and a kickboxer who is a second-generation Greek Australian, Con is warmly accepted into the Kerrigan family as Tracey's new husband. Well spoken, serious and polite, Con is frequently shown dressed in a parachute (nylon) tracksuit, popular in the 1980s but very unfashionable and associated with unsophisticated dress standards by the time of the film's release in the late 1990s. Con represents the large demographic of second-generation European immigrants living in Australia, and his marriage to Tracey reflects the degree to which these immigrant populations were integrating into the dominant white Australian culture at this time.

Dennis Denuto

Key quote

'In summing up, it's the Constitution, it's Mabo, it's justice, it's law, it's the vibe and, er, no, that's it, it's the vibe.' (Dennis, 0:55:27)

Dennis is the Kerrigans' family solicitor whom Darryl previously enlisted to defend Wayne and now enlists to help with his claim against the airport, despite the fact Dennis clearly lacks the experience or expertise for either case. Dennis is presented as permanently dishevelled and exhausted, dressed in a crumpled suit. While Darryl considers him to be 'the big artillery', Dennis' law practice is so small-time that he can only afford to pay an assistant for three days a week. Dennis is sympathetic towards Darryl but exasperated that Darryl wants him on the case; but, despite his cynicism and doubt, Darryl's enthusiasm wears him down and he agrees to help. Ultimately, Dennis comes across as a noble clown-type figure who does his best for Darryl despite being so clueless, and there is something admirable about his efforts.

Lawrence (Laurie) Hammill

Key quote

'Three degrees in the family! I'd like to see your pool room.' (Darryl, 1:06:01)

Lawrence Hammill, or Laurie, is a retired Queen's Counsel who takes over Darryl's case pro bono (free of charge) and becomes his friend. Lawrence's ability to laugh along with Darryl's initial assumptions about him is an indication of his lack of pretentions or superiority. Lawrence also shows his good humour when he agrees with Darryl's definition of QCs as the lawyers that rich people use. Lawrence recognises that Darryl is uncomfortable with Lawrence providing his services for free and, rather than making an issue out of it that could embarrass Darryl by revealing the large disparity between their incomes, Lawrence simply states he is in a position to do so. He is also diplomatic with Dennis; his facial expressions betray his bewilderment at Dennis' incompetence, and yet he remains polite and respectful towards him, and generously allows him to act as his instructing solicitor, despite Dennis clearly being incompetent in this area of law.

Farouk

Farouk is a Lebanese Australian who is a neighbour and family friend of the Kerrigans. His accent and slightly broken English suggest he is a first-generation immigrant, and the fact he needs Darryl to help him read the compulsory acquisition letter indicates that English is not Farouk's first language. Farouk clearly trusts, is impressed by and has faith in Darryl, which is demonstrated by him turning up to each court hearing in support of Darryl, and praising Darryl's efforts despite him losing the case in the Federal Court. Farouk represents the large population of immigrant labourers who live in the outer suburbs of big cities and who are striving to integrate into mainstream Australian society, but still misunderstand some of the nuances of Australian culture. Through Farouk *The Castle* aligns the plight and status of recent immigrants in Australian society with that of a working-class Anglo family such as the Kerrigans.

Jack

An elderly resident of Highview Crescent, Jack is another neighbour and family friend to the Kerrigans. Darryl is very caring and concerned for Jack due to his age and his vulnerable financial position. Jack represents the ageing population in Australian society.

Evonne

Another of Darryl's neighbours whose house is under threat, Evonne is first seen wearing a dressing gown and smoking; she is presented as a typical rough-around-the-edges suburbanite from the same lower-income demographic as her neighbours.

John Clifton

John is the council worker who does the original land evaluation of 3 Highview Crescent. Dressed in a plain brown suit, he is presented as a typical administrator who is simply doing his job. He is polite and respectful towards Darryl, despite being bewildered by Darryl's pride in what is, objectively, a low-value property. The fact that there is nothing distinctively threatening about John indicates that machinations to acquire the Kerrigans' house are happening at a much higher level; mid-level employees like John are just small cogs in a bigger system.

Ron Graham

Ron is the well-dressed lawyer from Hammersley & Laycock, the law firm representing the Barlow Group. While he is smooth, professional and polite when dealing with Dennis, his smirking and condescending tone indicates his contempt. Ron is used in the film as a contrast to Dennis, to emphasise the power imbalance between the Barlow Group and Darryl. Ron is shot looking taller and more dominant in the frame, with Dennis appearing small, dishevelled and slightly bewildered.

Sergeant Mick Kennedy

Mick is the police officer sent to question Darryl about the missing gate. It is clear that Darryl and Mick know each other, establishing a sense of mateship and the fact that Darryl respects the law, despite everything. Mick is both amused by and frustrated with Darryl, but also does not want to see him get into trouble.

Mr Lyle

The dismissive and condescending opposing lawyer in the scenes in the High Court, Mr Lyle speaks in a very pronounced way that projects a sense of elitism and superiority. He mocks the fact that Lawrence is invoking the Constitution in this case. When Mr Lyle criticises Darryl's house and then cruelly comments that homes like that produce criminals like Wayne, it leaves the audience in no doubt that Mr Lyle is the closest thing to a villain in the film.

THEMES, IDEAS & VALUES

The value of a home

Key quotes

'It's not a house, it's a home. A man's home is his castle.' (Darryl, 0:33:40)

'They're judgin' the place by what it looks like, and if it doesn't have a pool or a classy front or a big garden ... and because of that, it's not worth savin'. But it's not a house, it's a home. It's got everything. People who love each other, care for each other, it's got memories – great memories – I mean it's a place for the family to turn to. Come back to.' (Darryl, 1:12:18)

The major theme of *The Castle* is the idea that a house is not simply a building with a price attached to it, but a place into which people have invested memories, time and love in order to make it a home. A house can be bought and sold, but a home cannot. A home's worth far exceeds monetary value. While it is a message that seems straightforward and reasonable, and one that many audiences would share, it is an idea that has been challenged by changes in the Australian housing market over the past few decades, and by a widely held view of property as primarily a financial investment. These changes have led to a situation in which many people cannot afford to buy a house and therefore create a home for themselves.

The tension between the monetary value of a house and its value as a home is first significantly expressed in the scene where Darryl goes to see a councillor about the compulsory acquisition letter. He cuts through the councillor's bureaucratic language to get a straight answer about the situation, which is that, at all levels of government, there is an agreement with the airport commission that allows them to take his land. Darryl challenges this by stating that there is no agreement with *him*. The Barlow Group thinks financial compensation is enough to cover the expense and annoyance of moving, while Darryl wants to stress that the issue is that it is his *home* they are trying to take away, and that cannot be replaced with money and a new address.

Darryl's monologue in the presence of Lawrence and Dennis outside the High Court, towards the end of the film, reinforces this major theme: that a home is more than a building on a piece of land, and people who only see the monetary value of a house are liable to act in ways that hurt those who have an emotional investment in where they live.

Key point

The central message of the film – that a house is a home rather than something with only monetary value – possibly has even more resonance now than it did when the film was made, as entire generations are now priced out of home ownership. This is one of the reasons the film has remained relevant and beloved.

Social classes

Key quotes

'Would you stop pretending to be on my side?' (Darryl, 0:15:11)

'Three degrees in the family! I'd like to see *your* pool room.'
(Darryl to Lawrence, 1:06:01)

'It's called a home, you dickhead! And it's a bloody fine one. If there were more homes like that, we'd –'
'Have the jails full of people like your son?' (Darryl and Mr Lyle, 1:11:34)

The Castle is filled with visual and verbal signs that identify the Kerrigans as a working-class family, not only in terms of their socioeconomic status, but also their language, interests and tastes. An element of the film that some viewers found confronting at the time – and some still do now – is that, arguably, it invites the audience to look down on the characters and laugh at them for reasons that are closely tied to their social class.

An early example to consider is the scene in which Dale describes how much Darryl adores Tracey and is proud of her tertiary education, followed by a close-up shot of Darryl looking at her certificate in hairdressing. The joke is that 'tertiary education' is usually associated with a university degree, as opposed to a trade certificate. This could be interpreted as a condescending joke about a working-class family taking disproportionate pride in a family member completing a TAFE course. On the other hand, it could also be regarded as an endearing tribute to Darryl's pride in the accomplishments of his family, no matter what they are, and his ability to see beyond established notions of value or prestige.

Another of the arguably more condescending jokes in the film is the presentation of *Hey Hey It's Saturday* as the Kerrigans' favourite show, since *Hey Hey* was known for its low-brow humour. On the other hand, it is another example of the film's sweet style of humour, showing Darryl enjoying a simple pleasure and how his enjoyment is so infectious.

Another questionable moment is the conversation between Sal and Tracey about when Tracey plans to have children. Tracey says Con wants to start a family right away, but Sal tells her that she has her career to think of; this is a joke about Tracey being a hairdresser and its implication is that she does not have a serious career. On the other hand, it is a nice acknowledgement by Sal of Tracey's independence. The joke continues with Tracey saying she will not have children until she is 'at least twenty-three', to which Sal responds 'Times have changed' (0:27:00), implying that she had children at a much younger age. Again, this is a questionable joke about the perception that working-class women can only imagine having children early in their adult lives.

However, throughout the film there are moments that encourage the audience to share the Kerrigans' perspective, so that, while we are amused by them, we are increasingly on their side and feel empathy for them. A key early scene is when John Clifton does the property valuation. His looks of confusion, shock and disbelief as he observes the state of the property and hears what Darryl is saying about it create a scene played for laughs, and suggest how the Kerrigans might be perceived by other members of society – particularly members of the middle class. John is not presented unsympathetically or as a villain, but his work for the council will facilitate the property's acquisition so, by association, the film suggests that condescension towards the Kerrigans will align the audience with those who are trying to deprive the family of their home.

This is one of the subtle ways in which the film shifts from poking fun at the Kerrigans to encouraging the audience to identify and side with them.

The finale of the film, in the High Court, strongly addresses the issue of class divisions in Australia. The legal language and terminology used during this sequence – as well as the very formal appearance of the building and the other people inside it – demonstrates how far Darryl has come since the start of the film, but also that he is an outsider in this sector of Australian society. The fact that he does not understand much of what is said during the High Court hearing is another reminder that the legal system is significantly out of reach for people like Darryl, unless they are lucky enough to have somebody like Lawrence helping them.

The most direct attack on Darryl's social class occurs when Mr Lyle implies that the home Darryl and Sal have created has turned Wayne into a criminal. Not only is this the biggest possible personal insult to Darryl, since it is an attack on his family, but it also suggests that people from a more privileged class have a general disdain for and ignorance of people belonging to Darryl's class.

However, *The Castle* is hopeful about the potential for people to transcend class divides. This is manifested in the friendship that develops between Darryl and Lawrence, which culminates with the two men regularly going to Bonnie Doon together and Darryl placing a photo of the two of them in the pool room. Their friendship is another triumph in the film, as it crosses socioeconomic lines.

Key point

The heated exchange between Darryl and Mr Lyle during the High Court hearing is one of the most blatant moments of class prejudice in the film, demonstrating how one socioeconomic group in Australia looks down on another and does not treat their needs or concerns seriously.

Race and racism

Key quotes

'They say the plane, they fly overhead, drop the value. I don't care. In Beirut, plane fly overhead, drop bomb.' (Farouk, 0:35:22)

'What is it with wogs and cash?' (Darryl, 0:51:55)

An aspect of *The Castle* that may confront some modern viewers is its depiction of race and racism. The film acknowledges that many Australians have racist attitudes, and it often mocks those attitudes, but it also sometimes diminishes the harm done by those beliefs by presenting them as simply a characteristic of Australian identity that is more amusing than damaging.

An example of the depiction of racism in *The Castle* is during Darryl's father-of-the-bride speech when he makes a joke about Con's Greek family breaking plates (an old Greek custom). Darryl is deriving humour from a stereotypical image of Greeks, much to the delight of his family. The expressions on the faces of Con's parents indicate that, while they are not happy about being the butt of this cliché, they seem to recognise it is meant in good humour rather than as a deliberate racist slur. It is an interesting moment in the film that acknowledges the casual racism of the Kerrigan family and presents it in an almost affectionate way as simply part of their working-class charm. Twenty-five years later, it is difficult to imagine that a film would portray racism in this way and allow such an incident to occur unchallenged.

An even more uncomfortable moment comes when, continuing his speech, Darryl says most parents want their children to marry 'one of their own' and that the Greeks have 'a reputation', prompting an even more concerned look from Con's parents. In the narration, Dale justifies this by claiming Darryl's comments simply reinforce how much he has embraced Con and values Con's love for Tracey. Rather than letting Con's parents speak for themselves, the film reverts to Dale telling us that Darryl means well and we are mistaken in thinking otherwise. Although the scene is played for laughs, this is another example of casual racism being portrayed as affectionate and harmless. While displaying an awareness of underlying racist attitudes in Australian culture, the film when viewed today can be seen as possibly trivialising the severity of the impact of these attitudes.

Another aspect of *The Castle* that has not aged well is the Kerrigans being big fans of *Hey Hey It's Saturday*. In recent years this program has come under scrutiny for its male chauvinism and being racially offensive. The casual racism Darryl expresses towards Con's Greek family with his reference to stereotypes is the same style of 'humour' that was typical of *Hey Hey It's Saturday*, an attitude that was (and arguably still is) prevalent in Australian society.

The character of Farouk is used in an interesting way to comment on racism in Australia, especially when he makes a darkly humorous observation about the fact that, like so many other immigrants who have remade their lives in Australia, he has escaped violence in his original country. Australia has a long and shameful tradition of people in politics and the media stirring up distrust and hatred of various immigrant groups, so the fact that Farouk represents a typical Australian working-class person is a strong statement recognising that immigrants are an integral part of Australian society, as well as reminding us that many of them have fled war and terror.

The fact that many immigrants have been targets of racially motivated abuse is not something *The Castle* explores directly. The film was made before incidents such as the Cronulla riots in 2005 put a spotlight on racial tensions in Australia. However, *The Castle* does include a scene with Farouk that makes fun of stereotypes of people with a Middle Eastern background being violent terrorists, several years before the 11 September 2001 attacks on the World Trade Center in New York made this stereotype far more prevalent and harmful. Farouk reveals that, when a man came to his door to threaten him, he retaliated by saying he would get a friend to put a bomb under the man's car and kill him. The punchline is when Farouk confesses that he does not really know anybody who would plant a bomb, but he is Arab and a lot of people assume Arabs have bombs. The joke is therefore making fun of people who have bigoted beliefs about ethnic groups, and suggests that such stereotypes have little basis in reality.

It is worth noting that one of the people who contributed to the film's conception and writing (and was also one of its cinematographers) was Santo Cilauro, one of the co-founders of *The D Generation* and Working Dog, who comes from an Italian background. On *The Late Show* Cilauro participated in various sketches that made fun of 'wog' humour. While initially a highly offensive racial insult used in Britain and Australia to degrade people who were not Anglo-Celtic, during the 1980s 'wog' had been reclaimed and appropriated in Australia by performers of various other backgrounds, predominantly comedians, to create a brand of humour about their own cultures that was distinct from mainstream Australian comedy.

The relatively common colloquial use of the word wog at the time is reflected in the scene where Farouk tries to give Darryl cash for the lawyer's fees and Darryl says, 'What is it with wogs and cash?' (0:51:53). This throwaway joke may have prompted laughter from most audience members at the time as 'wog' was a term that was casually used and the joke did capture the tendency for many immigrants to still operate in a cash economy, as they would have done in their country of origin. However, today, it is unacceptable for people to use this word if they do not identify with one of the cultures that have reclaimed it from its racist origins.

It is also worth noting that the term 'Aborigines' is used in the film, but that is now outdated and not a term that many First Nations Australians find acceptable. However, in the late 1990s it was not widely perceived to be problematic by mainstream Australian society.

Anti-authoritarianism

Key quotes

'Darryl, they write the rules. They own the game.' (Dennis, 0:37:53)

'If you wanna take 'em on, do it the right way, by the book.' (Sergeant Kennedy, 0:49:58)

A key element of the Australian mythology of the larrikin is a streak of mistrust in authority; and, while there is little evidence to suggest mainstream Australians are the natural rebels they imagine themselves to be, it does manifest in a distrust of legal and government institutions. In the case of families like the Kerrigans, there is some justification for this wariness, which Darryl first displays when John Clifton arrives to value the property. This moment is played for laughs when it is implied that Darryl is trying to conceal that he has broken planning regulations by doing the various extensions and renovations to his house.

The car trip to Bonnie Doon reveals that the family own a police radar detector, presumably bought from *The Trading Post*. When the radar alerts Darryl to a speed camera up ahead and he then slows the car down, all the family look out the window conspiratorially. It captures their sense of defiance in having outsmarted the speed trap by spending money on a radar detector rather than a speeding fine. On the other hand, Darryl is shown to be mates with Sergeant Mick Kennedy, who is portrayed sympathetically in the film as somebody who understands Darryl's frustration and is really on his side. The authority that Darryl is fighting against is the indifferent political and corporate system, rather than individual people in power.

On a deeper level, Darryl's eldest son has been incarcerated for his involvement in an armed robbery, which the film implies was more a case of Wayne making some bad choices and falling in with the wrong crowd, rather than being a hardened criminal himself. Later in the film we discover that Wayne never received the kind of legal support that would have prevented him from doing jail time, due to the Kerrigans' socioeconomic status. Later scenes in the film are much more blatant in demonstrating how power and wealth enable some people to have higher and more effective levels of legal representation than people like the Kerrigans.

Justice

Key quotes

'Because this is an example of the individual, of how the individual, if he has the guts to stand up and shove it right up those people who think they can stand on top of ya ...' (Darryl, 0:32:25)

'What this principle [utilitarianism] fails to take into account, is that competing rights cannot be weighed one against the other.' (Lawrence, 1:10:42)

Throughout the film Darryl is adamant that his case against the airport is simple and straightforward, as in his view there is no way that his home can be taken away from him without his consent, no matter what the position of the law or government is. Darryl's attitude is naive, but it also articulates the anger of so many people when they feel powerless in the face of injustice. One of the challenges Darryl faces is that many of the people he deals with believe it is impossible for him to win. When Dennis says that it is inevitable that the Barlow Group will get its way, Darryl is infuriated, not only because the system so often allows powerful corporate interests to defeat everyday people like him, but also because people assume that such a defeat is inevitable.

Darryl's actions evoke the spirit of individualism, which prioritises the needs of individual people over collective interests, to ensure autonomy and self-sufficiency. This is a notion that in recent years has become increasingly aligned with the conservative side of politics, which generally aims to minimise government intervention in everyday life. However, in *The Castle* individualism is represented more in the spirit of average, everyday people being able to stand up against corporate interests, especially when those corporate interests manipulate the government and the legal system to get their way. Furthermore, the injustice of the situation is compounded by the fact that the motivation for taking away the Kerrigans' home is purely economic, as it is made clear that the airport could be extended on to other land without acquiring people's houses, it would just cost more.

Key point

The welfare of the individual versus the good of the community is discussed directly during the climactic High Court scenes when opposing lawyer Mr Lyle brings up the Tasmanian Dams case as an example of the court supporting something that benefits the community (for instance, by creating jobs) over the needs of the individual. Lawrence describes this argument as utilitarianism, which, very broadly speaking, is the philosophy that actions should aim to create the most happiness or value for the greatest number of people. However, Lawrence counters this perspective by effectively arguing that comparing Darryl's need to preserve his home with the need of the Barlow Group to expand the airport at low cost is a false dichotomy – that is, it erroneously assumes these are the only two, mutually exclusive, alternatives.

The Mabo case and native title

Key quotes

'Rent? We not only lose our place, we're payin' for someone else's. I'm really startin' to understand how the Aborigines feel.' (Darryl, 1:04:50)

'Well, this house is like their land. It holds their memories. The land is their story. It's everything. You just can't pick it up and plonk it down somewhere else. This country's gotta stop stealin' other people's land.' (Darryl, 1:05:03)

One of the most memorable scenes in *The Castle* is Dennis Denuto's panicked attempt to liken Darryl's case to the landmark Mabo case. At first this is played for laughs as the concept of likening Darryl's situation to such an important landmark court case concerning native title is absurd. However, when Lawrence appears in the film, the concept of comparing the two cases is then taken seriously. The film presents the idea that, just as it was an injustice for the European colonisers to claim the land belonging to First Nations peoples without any consultation or recognition, it is similarly an injustice for Darryl's house to be forcibly acquired.

Probably the most explicit scene in the film where a comparison is drawn between First Nations land rights and Darryl's situation is when Sal suggests they rent somewhere. Darryl is horrified by the idea, saying that the situation makes him understand the plight of Australia's original inhabitants. His outrage at the suggestion of renting also reflects the old Australian dream of home ownership, which was more achievable in the 1990s than it is now.

Darryl comparing his situation to that of Australia's First Nations peoples is an aspect of *The Castle* that does not translate well to the modern day, despite his good intentions. While the aim of the filmmakers seems to have been to demonstrate Darryl's recognition of the injustices faced by First Nations peoples resulting from their loss of land rights, today it comes across as a slightly disrespectful comparison, considering that, as a white Australian, Darryl is significantly more privileged than most First Nations people.

When Sal challenges Darryl's remark, he does elaborate, saying, 'Well, this house is like their land, it holds their memories, the land is their story, it's everything' (1:05:05) and Australia has 'gotta stop stealing other people's land' (1:05:15). Again, in hindsight this is perhaps not an appropriate comparison, but it does reflect the attempt some white Australians were trying to make in the 1990s to better understand and accept the impact of European colonisation on First Nations Australians.

DIFFERENT INTERPRETATIONS

Different interpretations arise from different responses to a text. Over time, a text will evoke a wide range of responses from its readers, who may come from various social or cultural groups and live in very different places and historical periods. Responses by critics and reviewers can be published in newspapers, journals and books, both online and in print. They can also be expressed in discussions among readers in the media, classrooms, book groups and so on.

While there is no single correct reading or interpretation of a text, it is important to understand that an interpretation is more than a personal opinion – it is the justification of a point of view on the text. To present an interpretation of a text based on your point of view, you must use a logical argument and support it with relevant evidence from the text.

Critical viewpoints

The Castle was a box office hit in Australia upon release and was also received extremely well by critics. While it did not have the same impact internationally, with some overseas critics feeling that the humour and references were too specifically Australian, others compared it favourably to similar low-budget feelgood comedies at the time, such as *The Full Monty* (1997) and *Waking Ned* (1998), both from the UK. Since its release *The Castle* has become regarded as a classic Australian film, with many of its catchphrases becoming part of the Australian lexicon. It was voted the top Australian film of all time in a poll run by the Adelaide Film Festival in 2018, and in 2021 in a list compiled by *Time Out* of the hundred best comedy films, it was the highest Australian entry on the list at number 26.

However, some elements of *The Castle* divided audiences at the time and continue to do so. This division was highlighted in an episode of *The Movie Show* that aired on SBS television on 13 April 1997, when Australian film critics Margaret Pomeranz and David Stratton first reviewed the film. Pomeranz described the film as 'a fable about an Aussie battler' and then commented:

> it takes just a little while to get rid of the niggling thought that these characters are being laughed at by the filmmaker, but then you're suddenly embraced by the enormous affection the filmmakers have for Darryl and his family. (Pomeranz & Stratton 1997)

However, at the time Stratton was not convinced, saying, 'I thought it was patronising to its characters'.

Stratton also felt that the film tapped into an extremely dated type of Australian humour, which he elaborated on in his review for *Variety* by describing it as 'a throwback to a school of comedy from another era, and a rather patronizing one at that' (Stratton 1997). In contrast, American critic Roger Ebert in his review for the *Chicago Sun-Times* found that the film's old-fashioned humour was one of its best features:

> It's about characters who have a rock-solid view of the universe and their place in it, and gaze out upon the world from the high vantage point of the home that is their castle. The movie is not shocking or daring or vulgar, but sublimely content. (Ebert 1999)

Ebert also focused on the family dynamic as being crucial to what makes the film so endearing and humorous.

The degree to which *The Castle* laughs at or with its characters has remained a major discussion point in ongoing analysis of the film since it was released. Writing in *Screen Education*, Brian McFarlane asks if the filmmakers are being 'clever and funny at the expense of the simple people at the centre of their film, and at the expense of some rather easy targets?' (McFarlane 2007). On the other hand, when revisiting the film for an article in *The Guardian*, Luke Buckmaster defends how *The Castle* 'manages to balance deprecation with tenderness and warmth'

(Buckmaster 2014). Aware of the type of criticism raised by McFarlane, Buckmaster elaborates:

> *The Castle* could easily have played as a down-the-nose ridicule of lower-middle-class suburban Australia. But [director Rob] Sitch avoids ridiculing his characters despite sending up the way they talk, the things they cherish, even the food they consume.

Buckmaster does not see any contradiction between encouraging the audience to laugh at aspects of the Kerrigans and also encouraging the audience to identify with them, arguing that, 'It is not the characters' plebeian behaviour that holds the film's focus but the sincere place from which it emerges'.

Similarly, writing for SBS for a piece celebrating the film's twentieth anniversary in 2017, Dave Crewe describes how *The Castle* 'at once satirises and admires its subjects, offering an enduring portrait of simple folk with big hearts and big dreams' (Crewe 2017). However, he points out that the film makes several assumptions about working-class life that reinforce stereotypes. Crewe also comments on the fact that the film portrays gender roles in a very fixed way, contains elements of racism (although framed as coming from a place of ignorance rather than malice) and is somewhat fanciful in its depiction of the crossing of socioeconomic barriers between Darryl and Lawrence. Most interesting is Crewe's discussion of contrasting perspectives on *The Castle*'s use of First Nations land rights as an allegory. He suggests that likening Darryl's court cases to Mabo potentially creates a false equivalence, but then suggests an alternative reading of this element of the film:

> Yet the film is ultimately intended to be a heart-warming fantasy, and while its allegory is imperfect, it might prompt a few audience members to rethink their opinions on Aboriginal land rights.

Two interpretations

Interpretation 1: By mocking its working-class characters, *The Castle* functions as a satire of the worst elements of Australian society.

The concept of the loveable larrikin, or its modern equivalent, the hard-done-by Aussie battler, has remained prevalent in Australian culture, drawing attention away from the fact of growing social inequality and racial intolerances. Even upon its release in 1997, the ideal that is presented in *The Castle* of an all-white family (with some token ethnic friends) happily living a working-class lifestyle in the outer suburbs was largely a fabrication.

In its opening scenes, *The Castle* almost immediately encourages the audience to view the Kerrigans as buffoons: despite living next to an airport, surrounded by large electricity pylons, on land with lead in the ground, in a ramshackle house that has decreased in value, they believe themselves to be lucky. The family's relentless optimism is an ongoing joke throughout the film, whether it is highlighting the woeful inadequacies of the house they desperately fight for, despite the offer of generous compensation for leaving, or their equally bleak holiday home in Bonnie Doon where their idea of serenity can accommodate the constant background noise of motorbikes, speedboats, electric mosquito-zappers or Con practising kickboxing. They have low ambitions, one family member is already in jail, and they are easily entertained by low-brow television programs, bland cooking and ugly pieces of craft. They reflect the disrespect for authority that Australians like to think they have, through childish and petty crimes such as ripping the gates off a private property or speeding when their police radar tells them there are no traps about.

Darryl employs the rhetoric of individualism when outraged that he might not get his way, but *The Castle* reminds us that only some parts of Australian society have the rights that white men like Darryl take for granted. The only prominent women in the film are the low-status homemaker Sal, whose main purpose in life is to look after Darryl, and Tracey, whose idea of independence is not having children until she is twenty-three and whose hairdressing qualification is one of the film's more belittling recurring jokes. Farouk and Con, the two major characters from non-Anglo-Celtic backgrounds, are both sources of ridicule for the way they speak and are on the receiving end of Darryl's 'good natured' racism: Darryl calls Farouk a 'wog' and makes fun of Greek stereotypes at Con's wedding. Furthermore, both Farouk and Con apparently need Darryl's permission to call him by his first name, which is not something required by any other character. Finally, *The Castle* reminds us how unjust Australian society is by invoking the long-overdue Mabo land rights decision, which Darryl offensively suggests is relevant to his own situation.

Interpretation 2: By walking a fine line between ridiculing and celebrating its characters, *The Castle* is a loving tribute to the unique spirit of Australian families.

Arriving in Australian cinemas a few years after the end of the early-1990s recession, *The Castle* was a much-needed affirmation of the values and characteristics that make Australia unique. By presenting audiences with the feelgood scenario of an average working-class family triumphing over the bullying tactics of a large corporation, *The Castle* presents an ensemble of loveable characters who reflect the best of the Australian spirit. By exaggerating the Kerrigan family's often naive and simple tastes and attitudes, the film showed Australian audiences of the day aspects of themselves or their neighbours in the characters, which enabled them to laugh along with them. Rather than being caricatures whose foibles are mocked, the Kerrigans are recognisably Australian characters whose ups and downs are presented with good humour and affection.

One of the immediate impressions that the film conveys about the Kerrigans is their ability to see the positive side of almost everything, considering themselves to be lucky when faced with situations that would distress or discourage others. Rather than being upset by the noise from the airport next door, the Kerrigans feel they are conveniently positioned should they ever want to catch a plane. They also find small and humble pleasures in everyday things such as a familiar meal, a home-made Father's Day gift or watching television together.

The most endearing aspect of the Kerrigans is their tight family bond. The characters are rarely able to express their emotions directly but the film constantly reinforces how much they love and care for each other. Darryl frequently praises Sal for simple things such as her cooking, and in these moments the film often shows us Dale's and Steve's content and happy expressions at seeing the affection between their parents. Despite him being convicted of a crime, all the family still love and support Wayne, making sure he is always thought of, whether it is through a present from Tracey after her honeymoon or the regular visits from Dale, who is so sensitive that he cannot help but feel sad for Wayne whenever the rest of the family are having fun without him.

The love and respect that the Kerrigans give to each other is also extended to the rest of their community. Darryl cares about his neighbours – helping Farouk translate a letter and helping Jack financially – and they all welcome Con into the family as one of their own. Darryl has more faith in Dennis than the solicitor has in himself, and Darryl also extends the hand of friendship across class divides to Lawrence. Finally, the Kerrigans recognise injustice when they see it, not just when it affects them, but also the historical injustices suffered by First Nations peoples, making Darryl one of Australian cinema's more enlightened leading men.

QUESTIONS & ANSWERS

This section focuses on your own analytical writing on the text, and gives you strategies for producing high-quality responses in your coursework and exam essays.

Essay writing – an overview

An essay on a literary work is a formal and serious piece of writing that presents your point of view on the text, usually in response to a given topic. Your 'point of view' in an essay is your interpretation of the meaning of the text's language, structure, characters, situations and events, supported by detailed analysis of textual evidence.

Analyse – don't summarise

In your essays it is important to avoid simply summarising what happens in a text.

- A **summary** is a description or paraphrase (retelling in different words) of the characters and events. For example: 'Macbeth has a horrifying vision of a dagger dripping with blood before he goes to murder King Duncan.'
- An **analysis** is an explanation of the real meaning or significance that lies 'beneath' the text's words (and images, for a film). For example: 'Macbeth's vision of a bloody dagger shows how deeply uneasy he is about the violent act he is contemplating, and conveys his sense that supernatural forces are impelling him to act.'

A limited amount of summary is sometimes necessary to let your reader know which part of the text you wish to discuss. However, always keep this to a minimum and follow it immediately with your analysis of what this part of the text is really telling us.

Plan your essay

Carefully plan your essay so that you have a clear idea of what you are going to say. The plan ensures that your ideas flow logically, that your argument remains consistent and that you stay on the topic. An essay plan should be a list of **brief dot points** covering no more than half a page.

- Include your central argument or main contention – a concise statement of your overall response to the topic.
- Write three or four dot points for each paragraph, indicating the main idea and evidence/examples from the text. Note that in your essay you will need to *expand* on these points and *analyse* the evidence.

Structure your essay

An essay is a complete, self-contained piece of writing. It has a clear beginning (the introduction), middle (several body paragraphs) and end (the last paragraph or conclusion). It must also have a central argument that runs throughout, linking each paragraph to form a coherent whole. See examples of introductions and conclusions in the 'Analysing a sample topic' and 'Sample answer' sections.

The introduction establishes your overall response to the topic. It includes your main contention and outlines the main evidence you will refer to in the course of the essay. Write your introduction *after* you have done a plan and *before* you write the rest of the essay.

The body paragraphs argue your case – they present evidence from the text and explain how this evidence supports your argument. Each body paragraph needs:

- a strong **topic sentence** (usually the first sentence) that states the main point being made in the paragraph
- **evidence** from the text, including some brief quotations
- **analysis** of the textual evidence, with **explanation** of its significance and how it supports your argument
- **links back to the topic** in one or more statements, usually towards the end of the paragraph.

Connect the body paragraphs so that your discussion flows smoothly. Use some linking words and phrases such as 'similarly' and 'on the other hand', though don't start every paragraph like this. Another strategy is to use a significant word from the last sentence of one paragraph in the first sentence of the next.

Use key terms from the topic – or synonyms for them – throughout, so the relevance of your discussion to the topic is always clear.

The conclusion ties everything together and finishes the essay. It includes strong statements that emphasise your central argument and provide a clear response to the topic.

Avoid simply restating the points made earlier in the essay – this will end on a very flat note and imply that you have run out of ideas and vocabulary. The conclusion should be a logical extension of what you have written, not just a repetition or summary of it. Writing an effective conclusion can be a challenge. Try using these tips:

- Start by linking back to the final sentence of the second-last paragraph, rather than leaping to your main contention straight away – this helps your writing to flow.
- Use synonyms and expressions with equivalent meanings to vary your vocabulary. This allows you to reinforce your line of argument without being repetitive.
- When planning your essay, think of one or two broad statements or observations about the text's wider meaning. These should be related to the topic and your overall argument. Keep them for the conclusion, since they will give you something 'new' to say but still follow logically from your discussion. The introduction will be focused on the topic, but the conclusion can present a wider view of the text.

Essay topics

1. 'Darryl Kerrigan's inability to view the world realistically makes him vulnerable to exploitation.' Do you agree?
2. 'Dale is a reliable narrator because he provides insights into his family's emotions as well as their experiences.' Do you agree?
3. 'Darryl's actions help to achieve justice and fairness for the whole community.' Discuss.
4. '*The Castle* encourages the audience to laugh at the characters, not with them.' To what extent do you agree?
5. Does the presence of characters such as Con and Farouk represent Australia as an inclusive society?
6. "But it's not a house, it's a home. It's got everything. People who love each other, care for each other, it's got memories ..."
'A sense of belonging is at the heart of *The Castle*.' Discuss.
7. 'Most members of the Kerrigan family struggle to reveal their true feelings, which makes the moments when they do express themselves all the more meaningful.' Do you agree?
8. How important is the role of Lawrence in *The Castle*?
9. 'Darryl is more opposed to the abuse of power than he is opposed to authority figures.' Discuss.
10. "If Dad is the backbone, Mum is the other bones, all of 'em. She keeps the family together."
'The family's wellbeing and contentment are due more to Sal than to Darryl.' To what extent do you agree?

Vocabulary for writing on *The Castle*

Close-up: a shot in which there is very little distance between the camera and the subject; a part of the subject fills the frame.

Cynicism: doubting or denying the goodness of human nature and people's motives.

Dissolve: an edit that briefly overlaps one shot with the next; the first shot 'dissolves' into the second.

Establishing shot: an extreme long shot that introduces the setting of a scene.

Fade-in: an edit whereby the shot begins by dissolving from black.

Fade-out: a fade whereby the shot ends by dissolving into black.

Flashback: a scene or scenes portraying earlier events than those depicted in the main story.

Long shot: a shot in which there is a large distance between the subjects and the camera; the background dominates the scene although the subjects are still prominent.

Medium close-up: a shot that has a comfortable distance between the subject and the camera; a medium close-up captures important details, but the subject being filmed does not fill the screen.

Medium long shot: a shot in which there is a 'natural' distance between two or more subjects and the camera.

Montage: a sequence of shots used to depict long passages of time. A montage sequence is traditionally composed of a series of quick shots edited together by short dissolves and accompanied by music.

Narrator: in a film, a voice-over that may or may not belong to a character; the narrator directly addresses the audience.

Parody: a humorous portrayal of something whose characteristics are imitated and made to appear ridiculous for comic effect.

Protagonist: the major character driving the story.

Satire: the use of irony, ridicule and/or humour to expose or mock human weaknesses and foibles.

Stylised acting: an unrealistic style of acting that is deliberately exaggerated or distorted.

Analysing a sample topic

'Most members of the Kerrigan family struggle to reveal their true feelings, which makes the moments when they do express themselves all the more meaningful.' Do you agree?

This topic is an opportunity for you to display your knowledge of how the film presents the characters and their relationships. It is also an opportunity to demonstrate your ability to analyse and write about aspects of the film beyond discussing the plot and dialogue. First you will need to consider whether you agree with the assertion that the Kerrigans struggle to express their true feelings. What evidence is there for this? What are the examples from the film to support your argument?

Your essay should then expand on how the characters in the film do or do not express how they feel, and whether the film represents this as a good or bad thing, or simply makes an observation. Finally, identify the moments where there are meaningful expressions of feelings and argue why those moments are important. The key to answering this question is to display a strong understanding of the film and how it has been made to elicit various responses from the audience. Pay attention to some of the smaller interactions between characters, which may not advance the plot or deliver a joke, but are there for the purposes of characterisation.

Sample introduction

> One of the most distinctive elements of *The Castle* is the strong bond between the members of the Kerrigan family. Both Dale's narration and the onscreen dynamics between family members make it clear how much they love each other, taking pride in each other's accomplishments.

However, when it comes to addressing serious issues, such as feeling sorrow about Wayne being in jail, or being worried that they will be forced to move, the Kerrigans conceal and repress their true feelings. Deeper moments of real connection do not come as easily as seemingly trivial interactions such as Darryl praising Sal for her cooking. However, when a character's depth of feeling is conveyed in a way that is unexpected or surprising, it resonates strongly with the audience.

Body paragraph outline

Paragraph 1: Identify evidence that the Kerrigans do not express their deeper feelings.

- Acknowledge that family members do express their fondness for each other, for instance through the recurring jokes of Darryl praising Sal's handiwork and cooking, and his pride in Tracey.
- Discuss how the affection between family members is identified by Dale in his narration, but rarely demonstrated on screen, especially between the three brothers and Darryl.
- Discuss the scenes in which Darryl becomes silent and deflects questions when pressed about sensitive matters concerning Wayne and the court cases. Also, mention the moment at Bonnie Doon when Sal hides her concern from Tracey.

Paragraph 2: Discuss how the film comments on their inability to express themselves fully.

- Look at the ways in which the film uses the family members' inability to communicate meaningfully with each other as part of what makes them endearing and humorous: for example, the first scene depicting Dale visiting Wayne in jail.
- Examine how Darryl's emotional repression has a negative impact on the family; for instance, during some of the dinner scenes Darryl's inability to engage with the family through the recurring jokes is upsetting, especially to Dale.

- Transition into examining Dale, by discussing the fact that the filmmakers present him as very sensitive. For instance, he often gets upset when he feels that Wayne is missing out, but is never seen to express those feelings to other characters.

Paragraph 3: Discuss the moments when characters are more vulnerable around each other, and why those moments are important.

- Argue that, because the characters do not always convey the true depths of their feelings, it is extremely moving when they do. You could refer to the scene in which Darryl is packing to leave the house and Steve tells him he has not let them down.
- Note that, when Darryl does finally drop his happy-go-lucky veneer outside the High Court and speaks from the heart, it influences the outcome of the court case and, therefore, the resolution of the conflict at the centre of the film.
- Consider that the most meaningful expressions of feelings are nonverbal: the film reminds us of this at the end, when Darryl and Sal look lovingly at each other across the room at the party.

Sample conclusion

> The Kerrigan family do not easily display the true depth of their feelings. The love, respect and pride they have for each other are evident, but the events of the film test their resolve to always put on a brave face. This means that when they do speak from the heart it carries weight and significance. Darryl's passionate speech outside the High Court also influences the plot of the film at a pivotal moment, further demonstrating the power of words when they carry emotion and meaning. Showing vulnerability may not come easily to the Kerrigans, but when they find the words to express their strongest feelings the impact on those around them, and on the audience, is both positive and profound.

SAMPLE ANSWER

'*The Castle* encourages the audience to laugh at the characters, not with them.' To what extent do you agree?

The humour in *The Castle* walks a fine line between ridiculing the recognisably lower-class Kerrigan family and encouraging the audience to affectionately embrace them. The Kerrigans may be exaggerated parodies of the Aussie battler archetype, but they are also characters that have been crafted to reflect the attitudes and behaviour of people who most Australians would recognise or even identify with. The filmmakers work to elicit laughs from the audience at the expense of the Kerrigans, but also want the audience to feel a sense of solidarity with these underdogs as they fight back against the corporate bullies who want to take their home away. So in fact, *The Castle* leads the audience both to laugh at its characters and to laugh with them.

The Castle initially appears to be a parody of the type of people the Kerrigans represent. Throughout, there are moments that suggest the film could be read simply as a long string of jokes about working-class bogans, who are endearing but ultimately not very bright or sophisticated. The opening montage seems dedicated to presenting the Kerrigans as loveable fools, highlighting Darryl's enthusiasm for living next to a noisy airport, the incompetent extensions to the house, Steve's ridiculous inventions, Sal's ugly handicraft work and Dale's simplistic narration. They eat basic food that Darryl is incredibly impressed by, they watch inane television shows and they have excited conversations about the most mundane aspects of air travel.

However, while there is much about the characters in *The Castle* that invites ridicule, the film never presents them as clowns or looks down on them. The house they live in may be in a terrible location, but Darryl's pride in it speaks to the fact that, even as somebody on a low income, he has been able to make a home for himself and his family; and the film suggests that to do so may have been a struggle. For a start, one of his sons is in jail, and having access to tertiary education has clearly not come easily to the family, hence Darryl's pride in Tracey for completing a certificate in hairdressing. What is remarkable about the Kerrigans is that, despite the clues in the film about past hardship, they are not bitter but in fact see the best in everything. As Darryl says to Dale, 'I reckon we're the luckiest family in the world.'

Darryl and his family are presented as underdogs whose situation in the process of trying to save their home becomes increasingly desperate. The film aligns the audience with the Kerrigans by showing us how kind and thoughtful they are. Darryl thinks nothing of helping his neighbour Farouk, whose first language is not English, to read a letter; and Darryl's concern for another neighbour, a pensioner named Jack, is sincere and generous. As Dale says, 'Dad also had a way of makin' everyone feel important.' Nobody in the Kerrigan family judges Wayne for his past transgression; in fact, Dale is so empathetic that he cannot help feeling upset at the thought of Wayne missing out on anything.

The family members adore each other and take strength from each other. These feelings are reflected in behaviour such as overpraising a home-cooked meal and going on a road trip to Bonnie Doon, a place that is objectively desolate but brought to life by the enjoyment the family members gain from each other's company and their positive view of the world. *The Castle* encourages the audience to feel such affection for the Kerrigans that, by the time Mr Lyle blames Darryl for Wayne being in prison, viewers are outraged at the cruel and insulting judgement.

The Castle does 'have it both ways' by expecting the audience to laugh at the Kerrigans, but then also to cheer for them. The aspects of the Kerrigans' lives that we laugh at are endearing rather than cause for derision, because we know they are idiosyncrasies of a family driven by good will and a determination to see the best in everything. The audience may laugh at some of the Kerrigans' ridiculous qualities, but ultimately the film asks the audience to laugh along with the Kerrigans as they find happiness in simple pleasures, in the quirks of human behaviour and in the failure of big business to deprive an ordinary family of its home.

REFERENCES & READING

Text

The Castle 1997, dir. Rob Sitch, Working Dog and Village Roadshow Films. Starring Michael Caton, Anne Tenney, Stephen Curry, Anthony Simcoe, Sophie Lee, Wayne Hope, Tiriel Mora, Eric Bana and Charles 'Bud' Tingwell.

References

Australian Associated Press 2004, 'Howard's battlers a broad church', *The Age*, 19 May, https://www.theage.com.au/national/howards-battlers-a-broad-church-20040519-gdxvk8.html

Buckmaster, L 2014, 'The Castle: rewatching classic Australian films', *The Guardian*, 4 April, https://www.theguardian.com/film/australia-culture-blog/2014/apr/04/the-castle-rewatching-classic-australian-films

Campbell, M 2006, 'Perhaps there's a little bogan in everyone', *Sydney Morning Herald*, 8 June, https://www.smh.com.au/national/perhaps-theres-a-little-bogan-in-everyone-20060608-gdnpim.html

Crewe, D 2017, '*The Castle:* cheat sheet', *SBS*, 10 April, https://www.sbs.com.au/movies/article/2017/04/10/castle-cheat-sheet

de Semlyen, P and *Time Out* contributors 2021, 'The 100 best comedy movies: the funniest films of all time', *Time Out*, 4 May, https://www.timeout.com/london/film/100-best-comedy-movies

Ebert, R 1999, 'The Castle', *Chicago Sun-Times*, 4 May, https://www.rogerebert.com/reviews/the-castle-1999

Kornits, D 2018, '*The Castle* voted Top Australian Film #YouMustSee by Adelaide Film Festival', *Filmink*, 31 August, https://www.filmink.com.au/castlevoted-top-australian-film-youmustsee-adelaide-film-festival/

McFarlane, B 2007, '*The Castle*: home of the brave', *Screen Education*, issue 45, pp.141–6.

Pomeranz, M and Stratton, D 1997, 'The Castle: review', *The Movie Show*, SBS, 13 April, https://www.sbs.com.au/movies/video/11685443713/The-Castle-Review

Stratton, D 1997, 'The Castle', *Variety*, 27 April, https://variety.com/1997/film/reviews/the-castle-2-1117341348/

Further reading: the Mabo case

Australian Government 2020, 'Eddie Mabo, the man behind Mabo Day', indigenous.gov.au, 2 June, https://www.indigenous.gov.au/eddie-mabo-the-man-behind-mabo-day

Australians Together 2021, 'Mabo and Native Title', 25 January, https://australianstogether.org.au/discover/australian-history/mabo-native-title/

National Museum Australia 2021, 'Mabo decision', 20 July, https://www.nma.gov.au/defining-moments/resources/mabo-decision

The Australian Institute of Aboriginal and Torres Strait Islander Studies:

- 'The Mabo Case', https://aiatsis.gov.au/explore/mabo-case
- 'The Native Title Act', https://aiatsis.gov.au/about-native-title
- 'Eddie Koiki Mabo', https://aiatsis.gov.au/explore/eddie-koiki-mabo

Further viewing

Bonny Doon 2012, dir. Matthew Saville. Starring Stephen Curry and Dave Lawson. https://vimeo.com/52208553 (A short film in which Dave Lawson and Stephen Curry – who played Dale Kerrigan in *The Castle* – take a road trip together. Lawson misquotes lines from *The Castle*, much to Curry's annoyance, then Curry gives Lawson some acting tips.)